SUREFIRE

Entrepreneur
MAGAZINE'S

55 Surefire
INTERNET
BUSINESSES
You Can Start for *Under $5,000*

Apparel and Accessories • Art Prints • Audio
Equipment • Automotive Research Service •
Baby Products • Business-to-Business Office
Supplies • Collector's Items • Comparison
Shopping Site • Consumer Electronics •
Custom-Printed Products • Downloadable
E-Books • Downloadable Music, Movies
& Videos • Educational Products • Event
Ticketing Service • Ezine Directory Service •
Furniture • Handbags • Health and Beauty
Aids • Homemade Crafts • Fine Jewelry • Ad
Network • Online Auction Site • Online Book
Store • Online Coupon Site • Online Craft
Supply Store • and Many More

Entrepreneur Press & Melissa Campanelli

The Surefire Series

55 Surefire Food Businesses You Can Start for Under $5000

55 Surefire Internet Businesses You Can Start for Under $5000

55 Surefire Homebased Businesses You Can Start for Under $5000

Jere L. Calmes, Publisher
Cover Design: Kaochoy Saeteurn
Composition and Production: MillerWorks

This publication is designed to provide accurate and authoritative information
in regard to the subject matter covered. It is sold with the understanding that the
publisher is not engaged in rendering legal, accounting or other professional services.
If legal advice or other expert assistance is required, the services of a
competent professional person should be sought.

Library of Congress Cataloging-in-Publication Data Available

Campanelli, Melissa.
55 surefire Internet businesses you can start for under $5,000 / by Melissa Campanelli.
    p. cm.
    ISBN 1-59918-261-0 (alk. paper)
    1. Electronic commerce. 2. New business enterprises. 3. Small business. I. Title.
II. Title: Fifty five surefire Internet businesses you can start for under $5,000.

HF5548.32.C3552 2009   658.8'72--dc22
2009006437

Printed in Canada

13 12 11 10 09   10 9 8 7 6 5 4 3 2 1

CONTENTS

CONTENTS

ACKNOWLEDGMENTS

This book could not have been written without Jere Calmes of Entrepreneur Press, who not only served as my supervisor, but also encouraged and challenged me throughout the process of writing of this book. Tricia Miller of MillerWorks was also indispensable. Together, these folks patiently guided me through this project and never accepted less than my best efforts. I thank them all.

Finally, I thank my husband, Rob Williams, who has provided support, encouragement, and laughter throughout this project, and to whom I owe so much. This book is dedicated to my children, Caroline and Christopher.

INTRODUCTION

I f you have picked up this book, you probably already know the internet offers a virtual universe of business opportunities.

There are many reasons to start an online business. First, online shopping is growing. For the fourth quarter of 2007, revenues generated by online-based businesses (and the online aspects of traditional retail businesses) were $86.2 billion, adjusted for seasonal variation and holiday and trading-day differences, but not for price changes, according to the U.S. Census Bureau (census.gov). That tally is up 4.6 percent from results for the third quarter of 2007.

Operating an online business also offers a wide range of benefits, including a worldwide customer base; the ability to operate 24 hours a day, 365 days a year; the ability to have a flexible work schedule for you and your employees; and smaller inventory requirements.

In addition, the business can be operated from almost anywhere: your home, a small office, or a warehouse location; One person can create a website that is as professional looking as that of a large, well established, multi-million dollar company. This makes the playing field much more level. An e-commerce website can be created and open for business in hours or days—not months or years—and there is very low financial risk (in the hundreds or thousands of dollars).

However, key reasons to start up an online business are the low startup and overhead costs. Startup costs can be as low as $5,000, and the business can be set up in a home office and attended to at night and on weekends, which allows new entrepreneurs to keep their day jobs. In addition, many budding netrepreneurs can set up their online businesses in less than one week.

TEN REASONS YOU SHOULD BE ONLINE

Need convincing that the web is the place for your business to be? It would be no sweat to list 25 reasons—even 50 to 100—but to get you started, here are 10 reasons why you have to be online.

1. **It is cost-effective.** The least expensive way to open a business is to launch a website. While you could spend many millions of dollars getting a business started, low-budget websites (started with as little as $100) remain viable business options.

2. **You cut your order fulfillment costs.** Handling orders by phone or mail is expensive. The most efficient—cheap, fast, accurate—way to process orders is through a website.

3. **Your catalog is always current.** A print catalog can cost big bucks, and nobody wants to order a reprint just to change one price or to correct a few typos. A website can be updated in minutes.

4. **High printing and mailing costs are history.** Your customers can download any information you want them to have from your website. Sure, you may still want to print some materials, but a lot can be distributed through the web.

5. **You cut staffing costs.** A website can be a low-labor operation.

6. **You can stay open 24 hours a day.** You'll be able to get your sleep because your site will be open even when your eyes are closed.

7. **You are in front of a global audience.** Ever think that what you sell might be a big hit in Scotland or China, but feel clueless about

how to penetrate foreign markets? The web is your answer, because it is truly a borderless marketplace. Watch your site log, and you may see visitors streaming in from Australia, New Zealand, Japan, and Malaysia—wherever there are computers and phone lines.

8. **You can save money.** A website can save you lots of money in many ways. For one, when you sell through a website, in many cases, you don't have to maintain a stock or inventory. All you need to do is maintain an online inventory that people can browse through and order from. Then, once they have placed an order—if you have set up your business this way—you can order the product and then get it shipped from the original supplier or manufacturer. In addition, if you transfer all of your business operations to your website, you don't even have to commute daily to your workplace; you can manage everything from where you live.

9. **There are no angry customers in your face.** You cannot ignore unhappy customers in any business; in fact, how well you deliver customer service will go far toward determining how successful you are. But at least with a web business, you will never have to stand eyeball to eyeball with a screamer.

10. **It is easy to manage your marketing.** Between your website and your smart use of e-mail, you would have complete control over when and how your message goes out. You cannot beat a website for immediacy, and when a site is done well, it is hard to top its ability to grab and hold the attention of potential customers.

You have other reasons to want a web business? Fair enough. The keys are knowing your reasons, knowing the benefits of doing business online, and being persistent through the launch. This road is not always easy to travel, but it is definitely a road that has transported many to riches, with much less upfront cash, hassle and time required than for similar offline businesses. And that is a tough proposition to top.

ABOUT THE BOOK

This book is divided into two parts. The first part explains the basics you need to get your online business up and running for less than $5,000. The second part provides an overview of the 55 businesses that are surefire winners.

However, keep in mind: Although this book does go into some detail about setting up an online business, its objective is not just to show the world how to start an online business. The data and information featured in each startup category are meant to give you, the reader, a "snapshot" or short overview of each opportunity. The book covers online retail sites that sell products, as well as sites that sell services and sites that offer directory listings and content.

Each listing includes four web resources. These resources are there simply to give you a research tool and help you find out more about a type of online business. You can use them to research a particular type of online business, get information about how to obtain merchandise to sell online in a particular category, or just view what the home page of a successful online business in a category looks like. Basically, they are included to give you the ability to quickly locate and compile further information about a particular online business opportunity of interest to you. And remember: Even though there are other online businesses in the category that you are interested in, there is always room for more.

Also, while marketing techniques are covered in Part I of the book, nearly all the business listings discuss marketing each product and service and how to reach and secure markets for them. Why? Because marketing is arguably the single largest business challenge entrepreneurs face, and often the source of the most startup funding.

Of course, there is no single solution to marketing something. For that reason, various options are discussed, and you are encouraged to seek out all cost-efficient marketing methods for your business, from using print and broadcast media to online and word-of-mouth marketing. In addition, most listings include the types of skills required to start the type of online business being discussed.

One note: While this book is all about online businesses that can be started for under $5,000, it is also about startup basics, such as buying a computer, setting up the site, simple marketing techniques, and common legal fees for setting up a business. As for selling merchandise, there are added costs there, whether you are making unique items to sell or simply selling merchandise. In general, it is a lot less expensive to start a services business than a product-driven one. In addition, this book does not guarantee that you will start generating a profit overnight, or even within your first few weeks.

As you would soon discover, once your website is operational, it would take time and effort to properly market your website, generate traffic, and attract paying customers. Your ability to earn a profit will be based in large part on what products or services you are selling, whether there is a demand for them, and how much competition you have.

Think you are ready to become an internet business owner? Prove it! Before moving on to the next chapter, take the quiz on the next page. Answers are true or false.

THE ONLINE BUSINESS QUIZ

1. I'm comfortable in a game in which tomorrow's rules are invented the day after tomorrow.

2. I see inefficiencies—waste and delay—in many current business practices.

3. I'm willing to delay this year's profits to potentially make more money next year.

4. I know how to size up customers I've never seen or spoken to face to face.

5. The net excites me; I honestly like surfing around and seeing what's new.

6. I can live with thin margins.

7. Customer satisfaction is the most important thing a business can deliver.

8. I'm not afraid of battling corporate giants.

9. I see opportunities where others see risks.

10. I am willing to work harder and smarter than I ever could have imagined possible.

Scoring: Guess what? "True" is always the right answer for any netpreneur. But you knew that already—because you are ready to compete in the exciting and fast-paced business world.

PART I: THE BASICS

I

GETTING STARTED

Now that you are ready to enter the world of online startups, it is time to take a step back and think about some important things you will need to do before you actually get started—and that includes writing a business plan and getting funding. This chapter will delve into these issues and others.

SOUNDS LIKE A PLAN

Since you are most likely exploring new territory, making decisions about technology and marketing, and establishing a new set of vendor relationships, a well-documented plan will guide you.

Why write a business plan? First of all, it gives you focus. By keeping a copy of your business plan handy, you can remind yourself about the goals and objectives of your online business. You have to constantly remind yourself why your website exists and who your target visitors are. When netpreneurs lose their focus, they often end up with websites that are too generalized for their target market—which makes the website's theme and subject unclear to new visitors. Also, whenever you face a tough decision about your website, your business plan can help you make a decision that will allow you to reach your goals.

Business plans also help you anticipate any problems your website might have. As a result, when writing your business plan, be sure to include a list of potential risks to the success of your website, and some ideas on how to combat these risks. Also, include a list of your website's competitors, if

TIP

What makes a business plan successful? In short, one that presents a well-thought-out idea, contains clear and concise writing, has a clear and logical structure, illustrates your ability to make the usiness a success, and shows profitability.

you have any. You can study your competitors in order to find their strengths and weaknesses and compare them with yours. When you include your weaknesses and potential problems in your website business plan, you will definitely save a lot of stress and time if ever you face these problems once your site is launched.

Business plans can help you to achieve your goals, especially if your plan outlines the necessary steps to reach those goals. Remember, real goals are not "wishful thinking." Realizing a goal involves a lot of effort. If possible, your website business plan should include operation manuals that will guide you with your daily activities. By writing down a well-conceptualized system, you would have a greater chance of achieving your target goals within a set time frame.

Your business plan should include your startup costs, in addition to your monthly and yearly expenses. This part of the plan will allow you to focus on the essentials of running your business and help you separate your luxuries from your needs. In the end, it might be much more cost effective for you if you stick to your financial plan, because you will not spend extra funds on mere "decorative" things that will not help you to reach your business goals.

The first step in writing an online business plan is deciding what kind of experience you want your online customers to have. Think not only about today, but also about two and five years down the road. Your e-commerce plan starts with website goals. Who are your target customers?

What do they need? Are they getting information only, or can they buy products on your site? These key questions, asked and answered early, will determine how much time and money you will need to develop and maintain an online presence.

Second, decide what products or services you will offer. How will you position and display them? Will you offer both online and offline purchasing? How will you handle shipping and returns? Also, do not overlook the customer's need to reach a live person.

Once you pinpoint a product you might be interested in selling, tap your skills as a web surfer and seek out websites and companies that are currently selling the same or similar products. Discover who your online-based competition will be.

Use search engines, such as Google and Yahoo!, and enter a wide range of different search phrases (using product names, product categories, product descriptions and company names).

Also, be sure to check shopping and price-comparison websites, such as Nextag.com, in addition to online-based mass-market retailers, such as Amazon.com. As you

TIP

If you are serious about the success of your online business, you need to find ways to give yourself every advantage you can over your competition. One way is to build a thorough business plan, a customized blueprint that outlines exactly how your business will succeed. This will give you that advantage, because business owners who don't develop organized and well thought out business plans—and instead rely on their senses and basic instincts—often don't see competitive risks until it's too late. Remember, the process of writing a business plan for your company can be a crucial step in getting your profits to where you want them to be.

TIP

Need help writing your online business plan? Try Business Plan Pro software (bplans.com) from Palo Alto Software Inc. The software has more than 500 business plan templates that you can quickly customize to match your business. Or you can use the software's step-by-step wizard to easily create a custom business plan from scratch.

discover who your competition is, spend time surfing their websites to determine how you would potentially do things better or differently.

In exploring the web for vendors to support an online business, have a clear idea of how to handle the "back end" of the business. A shopping cart program, a means of handling credit card information, and a fulfillment process are all necessary for selling online. However, a site can be more focused on providing information, seeking to promote offline transactions. This type of site functions as an advertising vehicle for you, where you do not sell actual goods on your site, but you use it to promote a services business you may be involved in. Your site may also be a content suite, where you offer information, much like a magazine, and support your business by selling advertising on your site.

The last decision is about promotional strategy, which becomes even more important when considering the millions of websites throughout the world, and the importance of getting noticed in that crowd of competition. The promotional strategy for your website is as important as the promotional strategy for your business as a whole.

GETTING FUNDING

Keep in mind that one of the beauties of starting an e-business today is that it does not necessarily require huge spending, considering that the technology to operate a website gets cheaper every day. In fact, as this book's title declares, you can easily start your online business for less than $5,000.

Where will you get $5,000? You will most likely bootstrap your online business by using your own money. "Financial bootstrapping" is a term used for several methods that avoid using the financial resources of external investors. The use of private credit cards is the best-known form of bootstrapping, but many alternatives are available for entrepreneurs. For example, you can take out a second mortgage or tap into personal savings.

While bootstrapping involves risk—especially if you are not a millionaire—the absence of any other stakeholder gives you freedom to develop the company the way you envision it. Many successful companies, including Dell, were founded this way.

SETTING UP YOUR BUSINESS

One of the steps necessary to start an online business is making sure that your company is a legal entity in the eyes of the government and IRS. So one of the first things you will need to do is to choose the legal structure for it. Aside from being necessary for government reporting and tax purposes, such a structure can enable your business to operate more efficiently.

In general, your business can be a sole proprietorship, a partnership or a corporation. Each has advantages and disadvantages,

TIP

One definitive online resource for starting a business is StartupNation's "Ten Steps to Open for Business," at startupnation.com/steps/55/ 10-steps-open-start-business. htm. The site covers the most important considerations when starting a business.

depending on the type of activity in which you are engaged. Your goal is to choose the form that works best for you.

Sole Proprietorship

A business owned by one person, who is entitled to all of its profits and responsible for all of its debts, is considered a sole proprietorship. This legal form is the simplest, and provides maximum control and minimal government interference. Currently used by more than 75 percent of all businesses, it is often the recommended way for a new business that does not carry great personal liability threats. The owner simply needs to secure the necessary licenses, tax identification numbers, and certifications in his or her name.

The main advantages that differentiate the sole proprietorship from other legal forms are the ease with which it can be started, the owner's freedom to make decisions, and the distribution of profits (owner takes all).

Still, the sole proprietorship is not without disadvantages, the most serious of which is its unlimited liability. As a sole proprietor, you are responsible for all business debts. Should these exceed the assets of your business, your creditors can claim your personal assets—home, automobile, savings account, and investments. Sole proprietorships also tend to have more difficulty obtaining capital and holding on to key employees, because such companies generally have fewer resources and offer less opportunity for job advancement. Thus, anyone who chooses sole proprietorship should be prepared to be a generalist who perform a variety of functions, from accounting to advertising.

Partnership

A business owned by two or more people, who agree to share in its profits, is considered a partnership. As with the sole proprietorship, a partnership is easy to start, because it requires relatively minimal paperwork and legal filings. The tax structure is the same as that of a proprietorship, except that the profits and losses of the partnership are divided into an agreed percentage by the partners. The main advantages of a partnership are that the business can draw on the skills and abilities of each partner, offer employees the opportunity to become partners, and use the partners' combined financial resources.

However, for your own protection, it is advisable to have a written partnership agreement that will spell out the specifics of the agreement. This agreement should state each partner's rights and responsibilities, the amount of capital each partner is investing in the business, the distribution of profits, what happens if a partner joins or leaves the business, and how the assets are to be divided if the business is discontinued. Because things have a way of changing and many people forget specific verbal arrangements over time, it is essential that there be a signed document by which all partners abide.

Partnerships also have disadvantages. The unlimited liability that applies to sole proprietorships is even worse for partnerships. As a partner, for example, you are responsible not only for your own business debts, but also for those of your partners. Should they incur debts or legal judgments against the business, you could be held legally responsible for them. Disputes among partners can be a problem, too. Unless you and your partners agree on how the business should be run and what it should accomplish, you are in for trouble.

In general, many experts say a partnership is generally the least advisable way to go. It requires filing a separate partnership tax return, does not carry liability protection for general partners, and can lead into legal and personal disputes. A corporate form of ownership is generally preferred over a partnership, because it can serve the same purpose while offering a cleaner and better-protected structure for the owners.

Corporation

A corporation differs from other legal forms of business in that the law regards it as an artificial being that possesses the same rights and responsibilities as a person.

This means that, unlike sole proprietorships or partnerships, it has an existence separate from its owners. It has all the legal rights of an individual to conduct commercial activity—it can sue, be sued, own property, sell property, and sell the rights of ownership in the form of exchanging stock for money.

As a result, the corporation offers some unique advantages. These advantages include limited liability (owners are not personally responsible for the debts of the business), the ability to raise capital by selling shares of stock, and easy transfer of ownership from one individual to another. Plus, unlike the sole proprietorship and partnership, the corporation has unlimited life and thus the potential to outlive its original owners.

The main disadvantages of the corporate form can be summed up in two words: taxation and complexity. In what amounts to double taxation, you must pay taxes on both the income the corporation earns and the income you earn as an individual. Along with this, corporations are required to pay an annual tax on all outstanding shares of stock.

Given its complexity, a corporation is more difficult and more expensive to start than are the sole proprietorship and the partnership. In order to form a corporation, you must be granted a charter by the state in which your online business is located. For a small business, the cost of incorporating usually ranges from $500 to $1,500. This includes the costs of legal assistance for drawing up your charter, state incorporation fees, and the purchase of record books and stock certificates. And, since corporations are subject to closer regulation by the government, the owners must bear the ongoing cost of preparing and filing state and federal reports.

S Corporation

If you are interested in forming a corporation, but hesitate to do so because of the double taxation, there is a way to avoid it. You can do this by making your business an S corporation. The Internal Revenue Service permits this type of corporation to be taxed as a partnership rather than a corporation. However, in order to qualify for S corp status, your business must meet the specific requirements set forth by the IRS. These include limits on the number and kind of shareholders in the business, the stock that is issued, and the corporation's sources of revenues.

The laws and fees for establishing a corporation vary by state, as do the benefits (legal and financial). The type of corporation you establish will also affect your personal and business tax liabilities in the future.

Another important step is choosing a name for your business. Once the name is selected, you will want to register your online business's domain name. You might also want to have a company logo designed. Depending on the business name and the unique look of your logo, it may be advisable to copyright and/or trademark your company's name and

TIP

To learn more about forming a corporation, visit Incorporate.com (incorporate.com) or MyCorporation.com (mycorporation.intuit.com). These independent companies can help you inexpensively complete the necessary paperwork and establish a corporation or LLC (limited liability corporation) quickly. Your lawyer or accountant can also help with this process.

TIP

To learn more about copyrights and trademarks, visit the United States Patent and Trademark Office's website at uspto.gov. The U.S. Copyright Office's website can be found at copyright.gov. The forms you need to file your patents, trademarks, and copyrights, in addition to directions and fees for doing this, can be found on these websites.

logo. You may handle this process yourself or hire a lawyer to do it. (More on selecting a company name below.)

MONEY MATTERS

Setting up a separate business checking account is an important step. Visit several banks and financial institutions to shop around for the one with most services for the lowest fees.

Depending on the turnkey website and e-commerce solution you choose, you may also need to obtain a credit card merchant account from a bank or financial institution, which allows you to accept credit and debit card payments online or by telephone. Because some of the turnkey solutions described later in this book handle credit card processing on your behalf, obtaining your own merchant account would not be necessary.

YOUR BUSINESS INFRASTRUCTURE

Putting together all the pieces for your online business infrastructure before you start selling products or services is essential. If you are not sure how to proceed with any of these initial steps, seek guidance from experienced accountants, lawyers, consultants, and other business professionals. A free source of business advice is the Service Corp of Retired Executives (SCORE), whose website is score.org. The organization, a nonprofit resource partner of the U.S. Small Business Administration, has volunteer (mostly retired) business professionals who offer advice and guidance to first-time business

LEGAL EAGLES

Covering legal bases is one of the more important things to consider when starting an online business. Neglecting the legal aspects of a web business could result in litigation or the loss of such valuable assets as a logo, brand, or website.

Unlike some assets in the real world, all the assets you purchase, create, own, and operate on the web to generate business and revenue consist of intellectual property rights, such as copyrights, trademarks, patents, and trade secrets. As a result, you will have to align yourself with a reputable lawyer, preferably one who understands intellectual property rights and the internet.

When you meet with your lawyer for the first time, you will probably discuss the basics, such as the company's organization and identity of the founders—and then delve into trademark issues, such as whether or not you have researched your business name to determine that the name is not in use already, and the importance of protecting your trademark. You may also discuss copyright law, patent law, libel law, individual privacy law, and trade secret law.

Trade secret law is particularly important for internet companies that have a new and valuable concept no other company has. In general, the law holds that if everyone who has access to your ideas signs a written confidentiality agreement that states they will not disclose them or use the ideas themselves, then the law will protect your ideas. A good confidentiality agreement should be signed by all of your employees, independent contractors, and even investors. It should be drafted in the very early stages of the startup.

The legalities do not end there. Web companies should also use web development firms to develop their sites to be aware of ownership issues. In short, internet merchants need to make sure that they (not the hired developer) own their website.

How do you find the right lawyer? Use your contacts or try FindLaw (findlaw. com), a website that not only offers names of law firms, organized by region, that specialize in specific issues, but also lawyers that cater to small business. You can access legal information on FindLaw that can help you run your online business.

operators and entrepreneurs. SCORE's website offers free online tools and resources of interest to new business operators.

In addition, the U.S. Small Business Administration's website (sba. gov) is an excellent source of free, online tools and information for anyone starting a small business. The "Small Business Planner" section of the site will take you step by step through the process of establishing the infrastructure of your new business.

Another free, online-based resource for new online business owners is Entrepreneur.com, which is maintained by the publisher of *Entrepreneur Magazine* and Entrepreneur Press. Click on the "Starting a Business" and "Online Business" icons on the site's homepage to start learning about how to establish your business. The site also offers marketing and advertising tutorials and advice.

CHOOSING YOUR COMPANY NAME AND REGISTERING YOUR URL

As mentioned earlier, you will have to select a name for your online business, and then you will need to register your website's URL (website address). This registration process takes just a few minutes and will cost less than $10 per URL if you use an internet registrar such as GoDaddy Inc. (godaddy.com). Selecting the name could—and should—take much longer.

Ideally, the web address you select should be easy to remember, easy to spell, and obvious to potential web surfers. For example, if the name of your company is "ABC International," you might want your website address to be "abcinternational.com" instead of "a-b-c-international.com."

Obviously, with so many websites already in existence, many website domain names are already taken. However, with more than 31.7 trillion potential domain names ending with the ".com" extension, there are still plenty available.

You can have many different URLs for your online business, all of which lead to the same place. So you could potentially register abcinternational.com, abcinternational.biz, and abcinternational.info to ensure web surfers will be able to find you.

If you have your mind set on a name that is already taken using

TIP

In addition to using a search engine to find websites, most web surfers rely on their common sense. For example, if they are looking for a company's website, they would enter "[companyname].com" into a web browser. Knowing this, you will want to choose a URL that your potential customers will be able to find by association.

the generic top-level domains (such as .com, .org, .net, .gov, .biz, or .info), you can use internet country code top-level domains from other countries. For example, instead of buyflowers.com, you can register buyflowers.tv, buyflowers.cc and buyflowers.ws. These domain names include internet country code top-level domains from, respectively, the Polynesian island nation of Tuvalu, the Territory of Cocos (Keeling) Islands, and Samoa. These domain names have been marketed as alternatives to the more crowded generic top-level domains, where the selection of unregistered domain names is much more limited. The .ws domain name, for example, has achieved some popularity because in this context it stands for "website" or "world site" rather than the abbreviation for Western Samoa, the nation's official name when two-letter country codes were standardized in the 1970s.

Most web surfers are accustomed to URLs ending with the popular .com extension. Ideally, you want your URL to use it. Otherwise, potential customers might get confused trying to find your website if it utilizes a less popular extension.

As you brainstorm the perfect URL, the part of the website address that you create can only use letters, numbers and the hyphen symbol (-). No other special characters or punctuation marks (such as !, #, $ or ,) can be used. Also, no spaces can be used within a URL. You can use an underscore (_) to represent a space, but this can be confusing to web surfers and is therefore not advisable.

The customizable part of a domain name and the extension (.com, for example) can be up to 63 characters long. As a general rule, the shorter the domain name, the easier it is to remember and to type into a web browser accurately. Virtually all of the one-, two-, three- and four-character domain names have long since been taken. Most important, the customizable part of the domain name you select must be totally unique and not be registered by another person or company. It also can not violate someone else's copyrighted name, company name, or product name.

Because domain names are not case-sensitive, you can mix and match upper- and lower-case letters to make a domain name easier to read and promote. For example, you could promote your domain name as "abc-company.com" or "ABCCompany.com" or "AbcCompany.com."

As you brainstorm the perfect domain name for your business, come up with a list of at least five to 10 options you like. When you are ready to register your domain name, you will first need to determine if the domain name you have selected has already been registered by someone else. This process takes under one minute. Simply go to the website of any domain name registrar, such as GoDaddy Inc. (godaddy.com), Network Solutions Inc. (networksolutions.com), or Register.com Inc. (register.com), and enter your desired domain name in the field marked "Start a domain search" or "Find a domain name." If the domain name you have entered is available, you will have the opportunity to register it immediately for an annual fee.

If, however, it is already taken, you have the following three options:

1. You can register an alternative domain name that is still available.

2. You can contact the person or company that owns the domain name and offer to purchase or lease it. Such a process typically costs more than registering a domain name that is not already taken. Acquiring a domain name from someone else or another company can start at $100, but may be as much as $1,000,000—obviously, if this is the case, you would have to consider option 1 or option 3.

3. You can register to be put on a waiting list to be notified when the domain name you want ever becomes available. The chances of this happening, unfortunately, are relatively slim.

After you have determined that the domain name you want is available, you need to register it with an Internet Domain Name Registrar. There is an annual fee to register a domain name. Depending on the registrar, registering a single domain name will cost between $5.95 and $39.95. Obviously, choose a company with the lowest rates. GoDaddy tends to offer very competitive rates for domain name registrations. In addition, this company makes the process extremely fast and easy.

Registering your domain name requires you to provide details about yourself and your company, including your name, address, phone number and credit card information (for paying the annual fee). The process will vary based on which domain registrar you use, but it should take no more than five to ten minutes to complete. After you have set up an account, registering additional domain names can be done more quickly.

Part of the domain name registration process most likely will involve providing the registrar with the Internet Protocol (IP) address of your web site, which your web hosting company will provide to you. You may also need to provide the Domain Name Server (DNS) numbers to the registrar; your hosting company will provide this information to you as well. In this case, it would probably be the company you select to provide you with an e-commerce turnkey solution.

Ideally, your website will have a single domain name that is easy to promote and to remember. However, because some people have trouble spelling or get easily confused, you might want to register multiple domain names with slightly different spellings. That way, if someone accidentally types the wrong domain name into their web browser, they will still wind up at your website. Think about the ways someone might misspell your domain name and register those domain names as well.

Also, to ensure you generate the most traffic possible to your website, consider registering domain names that relate to the products you will be selling. Think about the search phrases or terms someone who is looking for your products might use, and incorporate those terms into your domain name. This way, if someone is looking for a widget and types "widget.com" into their browser, they would find your website. Be creative as you register domain names; it is perfectly OK to have ten or more domain names that end up at the same website.

TIP

You can "park" a domain to reserve it before you have mounted a site. Many outfits tout that they offer free parking, but it's not exactly true: You still have to pay the registration fee. Free parking only means they will put up an "under construction" sign that anyone who hunts for your domain will find.

DOS AND DON'TS
FOR DOMAIN NAMES

Here are nine rules of thumb to help you select the best domain names:

1. Short names are best; they reduce the chances of misspellings and are easier to remember.

2. Avoid plurals, hyphens, and abbreviations unless they are part of your brand name or the correct spelling of a word.

3. The domain name should be easy to communicate verbally; it should roll off your tongue when you meet people on the street. It should also be memorable so they remember it easily.

4. A domain name should include your brand name and/or keywords that make your product easier for customers to find. Rather than a nondescript name, such as jonesbrothers.com, a better choice might be jonesbrotherssaddles.com.

5. A dotcom (.com) domain is usually the best choice, as opposed to a .net, .org, or other less popular domain suffix. Customers usually try typing a name that ends in ".com" first and may become sidetracked and go elsewhere if you are not there.

6. Names high in the alphabet help if directories or other services list domains in alphabetical order.

7. Be sure the name you choose is not someone else's registered trade name or trademark. Look up the name with the United States Patent and Trademark Office (uspto.gov) and your state's trademark database.

8. When you find your best choice for a domain, register it immediately, because someone else may register it if you delay.

9. Eliminate prefixes. Once on the web server, your webmaster can set up your site so when you type in the web address, you do not have to type in the prefixes of "http://" and "www." That will give you an advantage, because folks can find you both ways—"yourdomain.com" or "www.yourdomain. com." Those who do not type in those prefixes can also find the site and not receive a "site not found" message.

THE TOOLS YOU NEED TO GET STARTED

It is now time to outline the tools you need to move forward—tools to establish your business and get it online and fully operational. By defining your needs early in the process, you can create a preliminary budget more easily. Plan on spending up to several weeks laying the groundwork for your business and creating its infrastructure; this could be included in the design and writing of your business plan. Part of this process involves determining how your business will operate on a day-to-day basis, the tools and services that will be used, and the methods you will use to handle important tasks, such as credit card payments and order processing, if you are selling merchandise on your site. Because every company's individual needs are different, it is important to properly research and understand your options and then choose solutions that best fit your needs and budget.

THE EQUIPMENT YOU NEED

Because you are going to be launching an online business to tap the millions of web surfers out there, you will need, of course, a computer (PC or Mac), with access to the internet.

Depending on your lifestyle and budget, you may opt to purchase a desktop computer and set up a formal office in your home. There are many great deals to be had on state-of-the-art desktop computers from local computer retailers, office supply superstores, and online.

For a new, PC-based desktop computer, plan on spending less than $1,000, or more if you also need peripherals and software. Mac-based desktop computers from Apple (apple.com) tend to cost a bit more than PCs, but are still competitively priced.

Laptop computers, which are convenient if you plan to do a lot of traveling for your online business, cost more than otherwise comparable desktop computers. But they can be invaluable. Using a laptop computer gives you added mobility and allows you to manage your business from virtually anywhere that access to the internet is available. For a new PC laptop computer that runs Microsoft's Windows Vista (microsoft.com), for example, you will probably spend $600 to $1,500. A MacBook from Apple is priced starting at $1,100.

In addition to the computer itself, you will need to load your computer or laptop with business software. If you do not already have the core suite of applications you need, plan on spending between $500 and $2,500 for software.

Microsoft Office (microsoft.com) offers word processing, spreadsheet management, and a range of other applications. You might also want to invest in some accounting or bookkeeping software, such as QuickBooks by Intuit Software (quickbooks.intuit.com) or Microsoft Money (microsoft.com), to help manage your business's finances. The finance software you choose should be able to print invoices and packing slips for your customers.

Software that will help you manage a database of your customers, suppliers, and other important business contacts is also extremely useful. Microsoft Outlook, part of Microsoft Office (microsoft.com), Act! from Sage Software (act.com), or the Address Book software that comes bundled with Mac computers can be used for this purpose.

Based on what you sell, you might need to shoot and edit your own product photos to incorporate into your website. For this, you would need software such as Photoshop CS4 or Photoshop Elements (a scaled-down version of Photoshop) from Adobe (adobe.com). Again, depending on the tools you use to develop and maintain your website, you may need to acquire off-the-shelf website design and publishing software. Adobe offers products that are considered the industry standard for website design, creation, and publishing.

Another part of your computer investment will be in peripherals, such as a printer, speakers, scanner and a data back-up device such as an external hard drive. Prices vary dramatically for these items. To save money and desk space, consider investing in an all-in-one printer, scanner, fax machine and photocopier. For this type of machine, plan on spending from $150 to $350.

When it comes to internet access, you have a variety of options. You can have inexpensive dial-up access to the web for less than $20 a month. However, this kind of access provides a slow connection and makes it virtually impossible to utilize many of the internet's multimedia capabilities. Because you will be running an online business using your computer, you would be better served by obtaining high-speed DSL or broadband internet access through your local cable television provider, phone company, or internet service provider.

For a high-speed internet connection, plan on spending between $29.95 and $49.95 per month for unlimited web access. In addition to this fee, you will still need to pay a monthly fee for a turnkey website design and e-commerce solution in order to design, create and manage your website.

OTHER EQUIPMENT YOU MAY NEED

As you set up your online business, other tools and equipment you will probably find useful include:

- briefcase
- desk and desk chair
- filing cabinets
- floor and desk lamp(s)
- office supplies
- postage machine and postage scale
- printer stand
- shipping supplies
- telephone
- telephone service (including long distance, caller ID, call waiting, and voice mail, among other features)
- wastepaper basket

Your local office supply superstore, such as OfficeMax (officemax.com), Staples (staples.com) or Office Depot (officedepot.com) is a great place to shop for office furniture, equipment and supplies, although you are apt to find lower prices if you shop online. The Nextag.com (nextag.com) price comparison website, for example, is a great place to find what you are looking for at the lowest possible price—whether it is a specific computer or consumer electronics equipment, business tools, or office supplies such as ink or toner for your printer.

A WELL-PLANNED WEBSITE

What makes a good website? Before getting enmeshed in design details, get the big picture by writing a site outline. A well-planned site outline includes content, structure, design, navigation, and credibility. Keep these concepts in mind as you begin to plot out your site.

A web page is a text document that usually includes formatting and links to other pages. This special formatting is composed of tags, which are part of hypertext markup language (HTML) and are used to link one page, section, or image to another. Of course, you will most likely be using an e-commerce turnkey solution to design, create, publish and manage your website so that you would not do any programming.

For your online business, you will probably select a template offered by one of these turnkey solutions to use during the design process. The ISP that provides your e-commerce turnkey solution will probably have dozens, if not hundreds, of website design templates from which to choose.

TIP

Do not go crazy with colors—one of the biggest goofs of new web page designers. Stick with maybe two colors for type and use a simple, basic color for the page background (white, off-white, and pale yellow are good choices). Always test your page on a laptop with a very cheap screen—do not assume surfers will have high-end monitors. If it does not look good on a small, cheap screen, it is a bad page design.

After choosing a template that offers the overall design and color scheme you believe best represents your company and its products in cyberspace, you will need to customize the template and create your site. For easy implementation into your website, you will want to have all photos, graphics, and illustrations in a .JPG or .TIF graphic format.

THE 10 MOST DEADLY MISTAKES IN SITE DESIGN

Avoid these gaffes, and your site will be far better than your competition.

1. **Disabling the "back" button.** Evil site authors long ago figured out how to break a browser's back button so that when a user

pushes it, undesired things happen: There is an immediate redirect to an unwanted location, the browser stays put because the back button has been deactivated, or a new window pops up and overtakes the screen. Certain site authors are masters of this—their codes are often so malicious that frequently the only way to break the cycle is to restart the computer—and this trick has gained currency with other site builders. My advice: Never do it. All that is accomplished is that viewers get annoyed.

2. **Opening new windows.** Once upon a time, using multiple new frames to display content as a user clicked through a site was cool—a new thing in web design. Now it's just annoying; it ties up system resources, slows computer response, and generally complicates a surfer's experience. Sure, it is easy to use this tool—but don't.

3. **Failing to put a phone number and address in a plainly seen location.** If you are selling, you need to offer viewers multiple ways to contact you. The smartest route is to put up a "Contact Us" button that leads to all your information—mailing address, e-mail address, phone, and fax number. Even if nobody ever calls, the very presence of this information comforts some viewers.

4. **Broken links.** Bad links—hyperlinks that do nothing when clicked—are the bane of any surfer. Test your site—and do it weekly—to ensure that all links work as promised.

5. **Slow server times.** Slow times are inexcusable with professional sites. It is an invitation to the visitor to click away. What is slow? There is no easy rule, but any click should result in an immediate response. A new page or image may take a few seconds to come into view, but the process should at least start immediately.

6. **Outdated information.** Again, there is no excuse, but it is stunning how many site builders lazily leave up pages that long ago ceased to be accurate. When information changes, update the appropriate pages immediately—and this means every bit of information, every fact, even tiny ones. As a small business, you cannot afford the loss of credibility that can come from having even a single factual goof.

7. **Scrolling text and marquees.** It is an odd fact, but different browsers, as well as different platforms, do not display pages identically, which is one way these site-design tools get easily screwed up by browsers. Scrolling can also be maddening to the viewer who wants to know—now—what you are offering, but the information keeps scrolling off the page. Use these tools in personal pages—they are fun and add liveliness to otherwise static pages— but put these tricks aside when building business pages.

8. **Too many font styles and colors.** Pages ought to present a unified, consistent look, but novice site builders—entranced by having hundreds of fonts and dozens of colors at their fingertips— frequently turn their pages into a garish mishmash. Use two or three fonts and colors per page, maximum. The idea is to reassure viewers of your solidity and stability, not to convince them you are wildly artistic.

9. **Orphan pages.** Memorize this: Every page in your site needs a readily seen link back to the home page. Why? Sometimes users will forward a URL to friends, who may visit and may want more information. But if the page they get is a dead end, forget it. Always put a link to Home on every page, and that will quickly solve this problem.

10. **Using leading-edge technology.** Isn't that what the web is all about, especially when the number of Americans who have broadband at home increases every day? Nope. Your pages need to be readable with a standard, plain-Jane browser, preferably last year's or earlier. State-of-the-art is cool for techno wizards, but death for entrepreneurs.

CREATING YOUR SITE'S TEXT

If you believe you can write copy for your online business that will capture the attention of your visitors, effectively communicate your marketing message, and help you sell your products online, then by all means write your own copy for the product descriptions and other text-based elements on your site.

Your text must be error free in terms of spelling, punctuation and grammatical mistakes, and it should be clear, concise, and tailored to your specific audience. Make your copy inviting and interesting, but stay away from jokes and other content that may be distracting or quickly grow stale,

However, because your potential customers will rely on the text-based elements of your website, such as your product descriptions, to ultimately make their buying decisions, you might seriously consider hiring a professional freelance writer or marketing expert to create that copy for you.

A freelance writer, advertising specialist, public relations professional or marketing expert will have the skills and experience necessary to create well-written copy for your site. Plan on spending at least several hundred dollars to have a professional writer create product descriptions and other text-based elements for your site. An experienced writer will typically charge between $0.50 and $1.00 a word or quote a flat fee for a specific project. Avoid negotiating an hourly rate for a writer.

What Kind of Text Should You Post?

In addition to detailed product descriptions, a well-designed and professional online business will have other text-based elements that are used to educate the customer and convey your marketing message.

Additional text-based elements you might want to add to your online business include:

TIP

Need to hire a professional and experienced writer, programmer, website designer, photographer or graphic artist? The website eLance.com allows you to post your needs and have freelance professionals provide you with bids to do the work.

- company description and background information ("about us")
- press releases
- FAQ documents
- shipping information
- product return information
- customer satisfaction guarantee and customer testimonials
- contact information
- website copyright information

CREATING PROFESSIONAL-QUALITY PRODUCT PHOTOS

Photographs are becoming more and more important for online businesses. Since you are on a tight budget, you can use vendor- or manufacturer-supplied photographs of merchandise, if they have a selection of quality product images you can incorporate into your site.

An alternative is to research stock photo agencies for inexpensive, royalty-free images of your products for your website. To use these images, you will either pay a fee per image you use or pay a flat fee to be able to use an unlimited number of images from the stock photo agency's library of images. A typical stock photo agency will have a library that consists of hundreds of thousands of digital images you can download and use instantly.

The following are a few stock photo agencies worth contacting to obtain stock photographs for your website:

- bigstockphoto.com

- comstock.com

- fotosearch.com

- gettyimages.com

- istockphoto.com

- office.microsoft.com/en-us/clipart/default.aspx

- shutterstock.com

You can also create your own product images using a high-resolution digital camera and a photo studio you set up at home. If the products to be photographed are small, you can set up an inexpensive desktop photo studio for a few hundred dollars (plus the price of a camera). For products that are larger, you will need to use professional-quality lighting and backgrounds to create the high-quality images you need.

For professional and amateur photographers alike, the Canon EOS Digital Rebel line of cameras (usa.canon.com/consumer) are ideal for taking product photos to be used on the web. The Digital Rebel XTi, for example, offers 10.1 megapixel resolution and offers three-frames-per-second shooting with virtually no delay. Add a proper background and appropriate lighting, and with a bit of practice, just about anyone can learn to take high-quality product photographs worthy of being used on an e-commerce website.

For several hundred dollars, you can purchase the lighting and backgrounds needed for product shots. Lighting and background packages can be purchased from such companies as Photography Lighting Company (photography-lighting.com) and Amvona (amvona.com). eBay (ebay.com) and Craigslist (craigslist.com) are also great places to find used or close-out professional photography equipment that is on sale.

TIP

When taking product photographs, you'll want to use a solid color background. Depending on the product and how the photos will be used on your site, a solid white background typically works best. However, using photo editing software such as Photoshop CS4, you can silhouette objects and eliminate the background altogether, if desired.

Once you've taken your product photos, you can edit and manipulate them as needed, using software such as Adobe Photoshop Elements, Adobe Photoshop CS4, Apple's iPhoto, or Apple's Aperture, and then incorporate the images into your website. To learn more about Adobe Photoshop, visit the Adobe website (adobe.com).

YOUR COMPANY'S LOGO

All online businesses should have a company logo. This will establish your brand and make you look like the established company you are.

A good way to do this is to create a single- or multi-colored graphical image that establishes a visual icon to represent a company. A logo can also make use of a specific or custom-designed font or type style to spell out your company's name. Having a visually appealing logo helps your company establish credibility and recognition, plus it sets your company apart from your competition. Once you have a company logo created, you will want to showcase it prominently on your website, especially in the masthead area.

A logo can be created on a computer using graphics software, or it can be hand-drawn by an artist or graphic designer. Ultimately, the logo will need to be transformed into a digital image in order to be incorporated into your website.

Because your logo is an essential part of your company's branding and identity, you want it to look professional, be memorable, and be visually appealing. Ideally, you should hire a graphic artist to help you design your company logo, but that could be expensive. Try creating one yourself.

In addition to showcasing your logo on your website, it should also be used on your company letterhead, business cards and brochures, in addition to your online and print ads. It can potentially be used on your product's packaging as well, if applicable.

TURNKEY E-COMMERCE SOLUTIONS

With some startups mentioned in this book, you may be selling a service; building a content site where you would make money by selling advertising; or offering an educational or directory listing. You also may be selling a service, where you would have to take credit card orders but do not need a full-fledged online store. As a result, you may not need a turnkey e-commerce solution. If this is the case, skip this section.

Until recently, if you wanted to launch an e-commerce website, you needed to be a computer guru with a thorough understanding of HTML programming, Java, Flash and a wide range of other complex programming languages and software-based website design tools. You also needed to invest weeks, often months, in creating from scratch a website capable of handling the functionality needed to securely sell products online. Of course, a team of programmers and graphic designers could also be hired (at significant expense) to handle much of the programming for you, but as the website operator, you still needed a good understanding of website design and programming.

These days, however, a handful of well-known, established companies offer complete e-commerce turnkey solutions that allow ordinary people—with no programming or graphic design knowledge whatsoever—to use a set of tools and professionally designed templates to effortlessly design and publish awesome-looking and extremely powerful websites in a matter of hours—not days or months.

Best of all, many of these turnkey solutions have a very low start-up cost (often less than $100 a month). These solutions also include the tools needed to begin accepting orders and online credit card payments for those orders. In other words, you do not need to set up a costly credit card merchant account with a local bank or financial institution to begin accepting Visa, MasterCard, American Express, or Discover credit or debit card payments. This feature alone eliminates a significant barrier to entry that existed until only recently. Most also allow customers to pay via PayPal (paypal.com), an online payment system owned by eBay Corp. that handles all major credit cards, verifies their authenticity in real time, has no startup costs, no monthly fees, and charges 2.9 percent per transaction. Many online startups that are selling membership fees rely on PayPal. Google also offers a similar service, Google Checkout (checkout.google.com).

In general, these solutions—which are most likely offered by your ISP—include a suite of site-building tools; product catalog tools; content management tools; shopping cart technology; payment, shipping, and marketing strategies; tracking and reporting capabilities; and domain registration and hosting.

More specifically, a good basic turnkey e-commerce solution would include: preformatted storefront design templates that can be modified by selecting themes, changing colors and fonts, and changing the page layout within a point-and-click administration panel; a web-based store administration tool that allows you to work on your online store wherever you have an internet connection; integrated site search and browsing, which gives visitors the ability to search your online store by product and browse by price, category, and brand; and inventory management for all of your products.

The solution should also enable your online boutique to offer visitors product variations such as sizes or colors without having to upload each option individually; different category levels that enable users to search through your catalog easily; and real-time inventory control. It should also be fully integrated with a variety of payment gateways. Your site should accept credit card payments with a payment gateway (although this will require a merchant account) and PayPal; integration—with real-time calculations—with the major delivery service companies (UPS, FedEx, and USPS); automated tax rates and calculations; and flat rate and/or free shipping offers.

Nowadays, most solutions also offer search engine marketing and optimization tools, express checkout for registered users, the ability for customers to track and view order history, automated order confirmation e-mails, site reporting, free 24/7 customer service, and high-levels of security.

While most solutions offer the same features, before making a final decision on the solution you choose, make sure the e-commerce hosting provider offers some sort of scalability, so that when you expand—and you do want to expand, don't you?—you will be able to evolve your online boutique into a custom site without the hassle of having to switch e-commerce hosting providers.

In addition, before choosing a provider, remember that there is no better way to evaluate their services than to speak with their existing clients. Find out what e-stores and online boutiques are already up and running on the e-commerce hosting servers you are considering. Contact the webmasters via the "Contact Us" page and ask if they are happy with their current e-commerce hosting provider.

Then, whatever their answer, find out why. Ask how often, if ever, the server is down. Ask about help desk support. Most webmasters will be more than happy to proffer rave (or scathing, when appropriate) reviews of their e-commerce hosting provider. More than any other research method, this will help you choose what e-commerce hosting company may be right for you.

Many companies swear by the hosted solutions from the bigger names in web hosting, such as 1&1 Internet (1and1.com), Go Daddy Inc. (godaddy.com), Hostway Corp. (hostway.com), iPower (ipower. com), Network Solutions Inc. (networksolutions.com), ProStores Inc. (prostores.com), Verio Inc. (verio.com), Web.com Inc. (web.com), and Yahoo! (yahoo.com). Even retail giant Amazon.com is getting into the act; it offers a service called Selling on Amazon through its Amazon Business Solutions' offering (amazonservices.com).

The cost for these plans starts at about $30 to $40 per month, plus setup fees ranging from free to $50 per month. Some companies also charge transaction fees. Keep in mind that $40 will get you basic functionality; if you want more, such as promotional and merchandising tools and fully customized site design, you will have to spend a few hundred dollars per month.

FREE HOSTED SOLUTIONS

Yes, it is true—Microsoft and Google have launched beta versions of free hosted web solutions.

In 2006, for example, Microsoft launched a version of its Microsoft Office Live service that provides small businesses with a basic package that includes their own domain name, website, and e-mail accounts for free. The company charges monthly fees, however, for more ramped-up packages. For more information, check out the following website: smallbusiness.officelive.com.

Google also offers a similar free solution called Google Apps. It allows small businesses to design and publish their organization's website for free (but you bring your own domain name). The service also enables small businesses to offer private-label e-mail, instant messaging, and calendar tools to all of their users for free. Because Google hosts the applications, there is no hardware or software to install or maintain. Companies must submit a request to be a part of the beta. For more information, check out google.com/a/help/intl/en/index.html.

PRIVACY ISSUES

Because many consumers are concerned about their data being compromised online, it is a good idea for you to have a privacy policy—or a link to it—listed prominently on your business website and to openly explain it to your customers and prospects. After all, privacy and security—of consumers' information—are very important to online business shoppers. When they are buying high-end merchandise, they certainly do not want to have their privacy compromised or their data misused.

At many sites, getting out a privacy policy is as easy as putting a link at the bottom of the front page that says "Privacy Policy." When customers or prospects click it, they are delivered to a clear, concise statement of what information is collected from visitors, what is done with it, and if it is made available to other companies—which is not a good idea in today's environment. In fact, studies show that web users are especially sensitive when their data is shared with other sites or businesses. Most seem to feel that if they are interested enough in a site to want to hang around, revealing a bit about themselves is OK, but they do not want that information passed on.

Many online business owners turn to privacy promises developed by third parties, such as the Better Business Bureau Privacy Program (bbbonline.org/privacy) and TRUSTe (truste.com). Program mechanics vary a bit, but the essence is that a business site meets certain basic privacy requirements, pays a fee, and then gets to display a button on the website touting that it fulfills the program's requirements. Some users grumble that these programs do not truly guarantee privacy as much as they promise disclosure of what happens to information surfers reveal, but almost everybody agrees that they are a step in the right direction.

To sum up, you should post a link to your privacy policy in a prominent place on your site. In that policy, be clear, simple, and direct. A good strategy is to say, "We sell no information that we collect about you. Never. To anybody." Do not ask questions about visitors' kids unless there is a compelling and obvious reason to do so. And if you offer visitors free sign-up for e-mail newsletters or sales notices, be quick to remove anybody who asks—preferably on the very day you receive the request. Users grumble a lot about spam, and an easy way to win visitor confidence is to promptly remove anybody from any list on request.

Winning—and keeping—visitor trust really is not, and should not be, rocket science. Many of the same hurdles were overcome years ago by direct mail and catalog sellers. In the case of the internet, plenty of credit card issuers (American Express and Citibank, as two examples) are working overtime to encourage their cardholders to make online purchases with the full assurance that the card will protect them from fraud.

And in probably the broadest, most objective look at net privacy issues, the Federal Trade Commission (ftc.gov)—the lead government agency in the e-commerce arena—has argued that there is no need for government intervention to offer more assurances of privacy and that, on balance, the industry is doing a satisfactory job. For most site operators, this means do not screw up and you will be able to develop trust on the part of visitors. And once they trust you, they will buy.

PRIVACY PRACTICE

Not sure what to do when it comes to privacy issues and your online business? Then check out the interactive advertising privacy guidelines at The Interactive Advertising Bureau (iab.net) that were developed recently in a move to preserve consumer privacy. While they were written with advertisers in mind, online business owners can use them as a basis for creating a privacy policy.

Many online businesses turn to lawyers to draft their privacy statements. You may want to do that as well. The guidelines state:

- Consumers should be provided meaningful notice about the information collected and used for interactive advertising.

- Consumers should be informed of their choices regarding interactive advertising and empowered to exercise those choices.

- Businesses should implement appropriate information security practices.

- Businesses should be responsive and accountable to consumers.

- Companies should educate consumers about the benefits of interactive advertising.

SECURITY SEALS

There is another element that online businesses can add to their sites to build customer trust. Using security programs, often called security seals, proves that you are a technologically sound business that is not going to unintentionally let someone else misuse your information.

Unprotected small businesses face real threats from hackers and phishers looking to steal consumer data. Hacker Safe (hackersafe.com), Thawte (thawte.com), VeriSign (verisign.com) and its subsidiaries, including GeoTrust

MAJOR PRIVACY/SECURITY SEAL PROGRAMS

Program	Details	Annual Cost
BBBOnLine	Certifies that your business is a member in good standing of its local Better Business Bureau, and that your site meets set standards, such as prompt response to consumer complaints and adherence to the BBB's advertising guidelines.	Starts at $450
GeoTrust	Certifies that data transmitted to your site is secure and encrypted.	$249 to $1,499
Hacker Safe	Certifies that your site is tested daily against hacking to protect consumers from identity theft and fraud, and that stored information is encrypted.	$1,790 to $5,000
Thawte	Certifies that data transmitted to your site is secure and encrypted.	$149 to $899
TRUSTe	Certifies that your privacy policy meets set standards, which includes notifying consumers of how their personal information will be used, and giving them a chance to opt out.	$650 to $13,000
VeriSign	Certifies that data transmitted to your site is secure and encrypted.	$399 to $1,499

(geotrust.com), all offer services that protect customers' data, improving overall site security.

Because such security programs tend to cover specific parts of the e-commerce process—VeriSign, for example, encrypts data while it is in transit, while Hacker Safe protects data that is residing on your computer—businesses may want to consider applying for several.

Security-related seals are as much for your protection as they are for consumers'. In fact, less than 20 percent of consumers say they would shop with a site or company known to be a victim of a data breach, according to research firm JupiterResearch (jupiterresearch.com).

KEEPING FRAUDSTERS AT BAY

Many online business owners are concerned about fraud. Here are ten tips to keep internet fraudsters at bay:

1. **Carefully review orders.** Whenever you receive an order, review the order carefully. Make sure the consumer filled out all of the information correctly and that it matches. In most cases, you can catch anything that does not seem right by carefully reviewing the entire order.

2. **Check contact, shipping, and credit card information.** The consumer's contact information should match the shipping address and the credit card information. If it does not, then you need to find out why they want the products shipped to another address or have a credit card with different contacts. This is a very good sign of a scamster, but not in all cases.

3. **Use address verification services.** Provided by most merchant processors, you can run the AVS service on all of your transactions

to ensure that the information they gave you matches with informa-tion on file with the credit-card issuing bank. If it is different, then it is possible, among other things, that the consumer has a partner involved with the order. Contacting the consumer to find out the exact reason is highly encouraged.

4. **Watch for free e-mail addresses**. The majority of scamsters will use a free e-mail address to hide their identity. It is a good idea to require a real e-mail address from their own domain or their ISP when they order. This can be accomplished by stating the require-ment on your order forms.

5. **Document all contacts.** To give yourself greater protection and a bigger fighting chance against consumers, document all contacts you have with them. Keep all voice mails and e-mails, along with caller ID in order to prove your case.

6. **Check domain name records.** One little known trick is to look up the domain name records of the domain name that consumers are using in their e-mail address to see if it matches with what they provided in the order. This will only work if they have their own web site and used their own domain name as the e-mail address. Use Network Solutions' database to search for the records. The URL can be found at networksolutions.com/cgi-bin/whois/whois. Their information might not completely match up if, for instance, something changed or if they are using a business address versus a home address, but you should get an idea, such as them being in the same state or city.

7. **Watch very large orders.** Take special caution when receiving noticeably large orders, especially around holiday seasons. Also pay attention to orders that are sent for overnight delivery. Since the

scamsters are not paying for it, they do not care about the extra cost and want it as fast as possible.

8. **Use fraudulent notices.** Place fraudulent notices, buttons, and images on your order forms and your website content. Let the consumers know that fraudulent orders will be prosecuted to the fullest extent of the law. By having these notices, it will usually run off most scamsters.

9. **Do telephone searches.** You can purchase a database of phone numbers on a CD or you can use services such as anywho.com that will do a reverse search on a phone number for you. This will allow you to confirm the contact information for the phone number that the consumer has provided.

10. **Call the consumer.** The last, and usually the most effective way, to clear up all confusion is to call the consumer with the phone number they provided. If they gave you a bad phone number, then try contacting them by e-mail for a valid phone number. However, be very suspicious about this, because most people usually do not give out wrong phone numbers unless it was mistyped.

By using these tips, you should be able to lessen the possibility of that you receive fraudulent orders. If you are scammed, then take serious action by following the order and prosecute the fraudulent consumer.

eBAY

Before taking the plunge and starting a full-fledged website, many online business owners test the waters by selling goods on eBay (ebay.com) first. They have good reason: Today, the eBay community includes 84 million registered members from around the world. On an average day, millions of items are listed on eBay. "The most appealing and obvious reason a new business chooses eBay is the access to our enormous customer base," says Jim Griffith, dean of eBay Education at eBay.

To begin selling on eBay, you need to register and create a seller's account, then enter all the details about your item, including price, fixed price payment method, shipping cost, and a photo.

Griffith says listing an item is a five-step process that is pretty easy to complete. But he suggests you do your homework before listing items, such as researching eBay to learn what the current market value is for the types of items you are selling and what eBay sellers of similar items are doing on the site.

When you list an item on eBay, you are charged an insertion fee. The lowest insertion fee, for items with a starting price of less than $1,

TOP 10 REASONS TO OPEN AN EBAY STORE

Want to open an eBay store? Proponents say you should, because a store allows you to:

1. Control and monitor your inventory.
2. Showcase your merchandise.
3. Get your own private search engine.
4. Cross-promote your items on eBay.
5. Reduce eBay selling fees.
6. Become visible to search engines.
7. Learn from store reports.
8. Save time listing and relisting.
9. Get marketing help from eBay.
10. Improve your image.

is 25 cents, and the fee goes up to $4.80 for items that have a buying price of $500 or more. You are also charged a final value fee if your item is sold or purchased. Final value fees start at 5.25 percent of the closing value for items under $25.

Many online business owners—especially those already experimenting with eBay—are also turning to eBay for their online storefront services that allow you to sell your fixed-price and auction items from a unique destination on eBay. You can build your own eBay Store through an easy series of steps: creating customized categories, including your own logo or choosing one of eBay's online images, and listing item descriptions and policies.

An eBay Store is promoted to eBay users in several ways: All your listings contain an eBay Store "red door" icon that invites buyers to visit your eBay Store. The eBay Store icon is attached to your user ID for extra visibility. Buyers are also driven to your store through the eBay Store Directory, which is designed to promote all stores. And you receive your own personalized eBay Store website address to distribute and promote. There are three levels for stores, ranging from $15.95 to $299.95 a month.

WEB MARKETING TACTICS

This chapter will cover some of the most common forms of online marketing today, including search engine optimization, search engine marketing, comparison shopping sites, online display advertising, and affiliate marketing programs, among other tactics. In order to be a successful online business owner today, you will have to be familiar with some, if not all, of these techniques.

SEARCH ENGINE OPTIMIZATION

Search engine optimization (SEO) is essential for your online startup. Search engine optimization involves registering your site with major search engines, such as Google (google.com) and Yahoo! (yahoo.com), and then working to constantly maintain and improve your ranking/positioning with each search engine so your site is easy to find and receives top placement.

The first step is to register your website with the major search engines. This can be done, one at a time, by manually visiting each search engine and completing a new website recommendation form. The process is time consuming and often confusing. An alternative is to pay a third-party submission service to register your site with hundreds of the popular search engines simultaneously.

In addition to accepting submissions from website operators, many search engines and web directories use automated "spiders" or "crawlers" to continuously search the web and gather details about new websites (and updates to existing sites). How these automatic listings are gathered, cataloged, and categorized is based in large part on how your website uses meta tags and keywords throughout the site.

Meta Tags

Meta tags have three parts: the title of your site, a description, and a list of keywords. The information you provide (by incorporating it into your site's HTML programming) is used to categorize your site's content appropriately. In addition to the site's description, title, and list of relevant keywords within its HTML programming, you will need to incorporate a text-based description of your site, which also uses keywords to describe your site's content.

The better planned and more comprehensive your meta tags are, the more traffic you will ultimately generate to your site once it gets added to a search engine. Experts say the description should be a sentence or two that describes the content of the web page, and it should use the main keywords and key phrases found on this page. In addition, the maximum number of characters should be 255.

If your e-commerce turnkey solution does not automatically incorporate meta tags into your website, there are many free online tools that allow you to create them and the appropriate HTML programming. You then cut and paste these lines of programming into your site with ease. No programming knowledge is required. To find these tools, do a simple search of the phrase "meta tag creation."

● TIP

Want to learn more about how to use meta tags? Check out the following link: searchenginewatch.com.

HIGH RANKINGS

After your site gets listed with a search engine and appears when searches are conducted by surfers, you then must keep your listing up-to-date and take whatever steps are possible to maintain and improve your listing.

Meta tags can help you score high rankings, but perhaps the best way to score high in search engines is to have good, solid content, especially with regard to the terms for which you want to be found. Experts say it is also important to continually add new content to your site.

Good page titles are extremely helpful. A good page title usually includes five to eight words per page and does not include filler words such as "the," "and," and "a," which are the most common examples. Remember: Because a page title will appear hyperlinked on the search engines when your page is found, you should entice searchers to click on the title by making it a bit provocative. The best way to do this is to use some descriptive keywords along with your business name. The words people are most likely to search should appear first in the title (this is called "keyword prominence"). Other tips:

- Make sure your keywords are in your page headline and subheads.

- Make sure keywords are in the first paragraph of your body text.

- Use keywords in hyperlinks.

- Make your navigation system search engine friendly.

- Develop several pages focused on particular keywords.

SEO can be a time-consuming process you do yourself, or you can hire an SEO expert to handle it on your behalf, which will probably generate better results faster. If you want or need to have a listing for your site appear on the search engines quickly (as in within hours, not weeks), seriously consider using paid search engine marketing programs to supplement your free listings. We discuss these programs below.

SEARCH ENGINE MARKETING

Many online startups also invest in search engine marketing programs that allow them to pay to place their sites in the top results of search engines. Basically, every major search engine accepts paid listings—also known as "pay-per-click programs"—that are usually marked as "Sponsored Links" on the websites.

These programs allow you to bid on the terms for which you wish to appear. You then agree to pay a certain amount each time someone clicks on your listing. Costs for pay-for-placement start around a nickel a click and go up considerably based on how high you want your site to appear—and competition for keywords has the biggest bearing on that. For example, a bid on "jewelry" will result in payment of a few

SUBMIT YOUR SITE TO ONLINE DIRECTORIES

Try submitting your site to online directories, because listings in these directories help search engines such as Google find, index, and rank your site. Your first step should be to list your site for free in the Open Directory Project (dmoz.com), which is overseen by thousands of human editors. You also may want to try Yahoo! Directory Submit service (docs.yahoo.com/info/suggest/submit.html). For a $299 annual fee, Yahoo! guarantees that within seven business days, a member of Yahoo!'s editorial staff will look at your site and consider it for inclusion in the Yahoo! Directory. Just keep in mind that payment does not automatically guarantee inclusion in the directory or site placement.

bucks a click if you want to get on the first page of results. But if you are promoting say, pearl necklaces, you may be able to get on top paying just a dime a click.

Key programs are from Google (Google AdWords program; adwords. google.com), MSN Search (Microsoft adCenter; adcenter.microsoft.com), and Yahoo! (Yahoo! Sponsored Search, a service offering from Yahoo! Search Marketing; searchmarketing.yahoo.com). These programs charge a nominal fee to get started.

One of the best things about Search Engine Marketing (SEM) campaigns is that they can be created and launched with a very low budget. At least initially, you will probably want to experiment with a few different ad variations and keyword lists until you create an ad that has a low cost per click and high click-through rate. Once you have formulated one or more ads that generate results, then you should invest hundreds or thousands of dollars into that ad campaign. Spending thousands on a campaign that ultimately generates poor results wastes your money and does not generate the traffic to your site that you want and need.

Although there are myriad choices out there and the concepts may seem confusing, many online startups swear by paid search programs. As long as you plan your campaigns carefully, budget properly, and read the fine print, they can really help you improve your reach.

Lord of the Rings

Another marketing technique you might want to think about is participating in a webring. Generally speaking, a webring is a collection of websites that is joined together in a circular structure. When used to improve search engine rankings, webrings can be considered an SEO technique.

To be a part of the webring, each site has a common navigation bar that contains links to the previous and next site. By clicking next (or previous) repeatedly, the surfer will eventually reach the site where they began; this is the origin of the term webring.

However, the click-through route around the ring is usually supplemented by a central site with links to all member sites; this prevents the ring from breaking if a member site goes offline.

Webrings are usually organized around a specific theme, often educational or social. Webrings usually have a moderator who decides which pages to include. After approval, webmasters add their pages to the ring by "linking in;" this process requires adding the necessary HTML or JavaScript to their site. Try it—you might like it.

COMPARISON SHOPPING SITES

Attracting qualified traffic, people who are already interested in buying your product or service, is fundamental to your success. That is why online business owners should know about comparison shopping sites, also known as "shopping bots." Shopping bots are similar to search engines, except that instead of finding information, they help shoppers find the products or services they are seeking.

Shopping bot sites list specific product information so that shoppers can compare features and prices. This feature means that shopping bots can be an excellent way for your potential customers to find out exactly what you have to offer—and how to get it. Best of all, shopping bots can be a great place for business owners who are struggling to stand out in competitive markets to capture the eyeballs of qualified potential customers. Best of all, shopping bots are a less expensive alternative to the more popular pay-per-click ads like those from Google AdWords.

Though shopping bot sites differ slightly from each other, registering your site and products with most of them is usually pretty easy. In terms of cost, some work on a pay-per-click basis, while others expect a commission on the sale and, sometimes, a listing fee. Which sites are the leaders? Try AOL Shopping (shopping.aol.com), BizRate (bizrate. com), Google Product Search (google.com/products), NexTag (nextag. com), PriceGrabber (pricegrabber.com), Shopping.com (shopping. com), Shopzilla.com (shopzilla.com), and Yahoo! Shopping (shopping. yahoo.com).

The drawback of these sites, however, is that the potential customer will oftentimes be looking for the lowest price possible, and if you are not offering it, they will simply shop elsewhere. But if the products you are selling have a high profit margin, or you are willing to compete with countless other online merchants based mainly on price, price comparison websites can be an extremely viable sales tool.

This type of service also benefits merchants that focus on providing top-notch customer service, because the majority of these comparison shopping sites display customer ratings or rankings. A savvy web shopper will know to visit an online merchant that has both the lowest price and the best customer feedback, all of which is displayed when they use a comparison shopping site.

OTHER LINKING STRATEGIES

SEO, SEM and comparison-shopping sites are key ways to get online shoppers to link to your e-boutique. There are other linking strategies as well; however, you would be wise to place the links to other sites on an out-of-the-way page on your site, so that you do not send people to another site after working so hard to get them to yours.

You also may want to write articles in your area of expertise and distribute them to editors as free content for their e-mail newsletters or on their websites. For example, if you are an expert on pearl jewelry, you can write an article for a jewelry publication that includes tips on how to choose the best pearl necklaces to buy or sell. Just ask that a link to your website and/or a description of your site be included with the article.

Another key way to draw attention to your online business is to use public relations tactics such as releasing press releases to web-based periodicals in your industry or to press release websites. Some leading PR websites include 24-7 Press Release (24-7pressrelease.com), Marketwire (marketwire.com), PRBuzz.com (prbuzz.com), and PRWeb (prweb.com). Placing your online business's URL in online copies of your press releases also increases link popularity.

In general, SEO and linking strategies can be a great, inexpensive way to get the word out about your online business.

ONLINE DISPLAY ADVERTISING

Another tactic you may want to use to get visitors to your online business is online display advertising, which allows you to purchase ad space on other websites that might appeal to your target audience. Your ads can incorporate text, graphics, animation, sound, and even video to convey your marketing message. Unlike traditional print ads, however, web users who see your online display ad can simply click on the ad and be transferred to your website in seconds in order to gather more information or to make a purchase.

Running online display ads on popular websites costs significantly more than using SEM ads. What your ad says and the visual elements used to convey the message (the overall look of the ad) are equally important. Thus, in addition to spending more to display your ads, you will probably want to hire a professional advertising agency or graphic artist to design the ads themselves to ensure they look professional and are visually appealing.

Depending on where you want your online display ads to appear, size requirements, ad content specifications, and how much you pay will vary dramatically. In addition to choosing appropriate websites for your ads, you will need to select the exact placement of your ad on each website's page. Online real estate has value, based on the potential number of people who will be seeing the ad and the physical size of the ad (which is measured in pixels).

In general, the more people who might see your ad, the higher the ad rates will be. Depending on the website, however, you may have to pay based on overall impressions (the number of people who simply see your ad), or you may only be responsible for paying a predetermined fee only when people click on your ad. Another alternative is to pay a commission when a website referral results in a sale. The payment terms are typically created by the individual website.

The best way to find websites to advertise on is to put yourself in your target customer's shoes and begin surfing the web in search of sites that offer content that is appealing. Next, determine if those sites accept display advertising, and request advertising information if they do. Sites that accept display ads typically have a link on the home page that says "Advertise Here" or "Advertising Information."

AFFILIATE MARKETING PROGRAMS

Want to immediately generate cash from your online business? Try an affiliate marketing program. From Amazon to OfficeMax, leading online retailers are eager to pay you for driving sales their way. How? By putting their link—such as a banner or text—on your site.

For every click-through that results in a sale, you earn a commission, anywhere from 1 to 10 percent for multi-channel retailers, or 30 to 50 percent in the software sector. In some cases, you can collect a commission on all sales that take place up to 10 days after you send someone to a site. For example, if a customer visits your site and clicks on the leading online company's banner ad and does not buy anything right away but purchases something a few days later, you will still get credit for the sale.

In some cases, you are compensated even if the visitor does not buy anything. You are paid just for having driven traffic to the merchant's site. This method is not as popular as the former programs, however. The affiliate's reward varies from merchant to merchant and program to program, depending on the terms of the merchant's offer.

There are many independent, third-party affiliate program agencies that will help you create and manage your program. Using any search engine, enter the search phrase, "Affiliate Marketing" or "Affiliate Program." LinkShare (linkshare.com) continues to be an industry leader when it comes to administering an affiliate program. Other companies include Associate Programs (associateprograms.com), Click Booth (click-booth.com), Commission Junction (cj.com), and Commission Soup (commissionsoup.com).

Supposedly, the idea for affiliate programs—where big merchants enlist small sites as a de facto sales force—got its start in 1996 when a woman talking with Amazon.com founder Jeff Bezos at a cocktail party asked how she might sell books about divorce on her website. Bezos noodled the idea, and a light bulb went on. He realized the potential benefits to both were great, and the result was the launch of Amazon's affiliate program, one of the industry's most successful.

The primary appeal of affiliate marketing is the fact that it is always tied to performance. Marketers are not paying for relationships or placements that do not work. It is not without risk, nor is it always the most cost-effective in the long term, but dollar for dollar, it is usually a good investment.

How big is affiliate marketing? Although it is not as big a part of their overall sales and marketing program as paid search or e-mail, affiliate marketing is an effective strategy to build broader brand awareness and drive motivated buyers to business-to-consumer e-commerce sites, say web retailers participating in the latest Internet Retailer (internetretailer.com) survey.

Most web retailers have already made a multiyear investment in affiliate marketing and count on a network of several thousand affili-

TIP

The information and message communicated in all of your advertising, marketing, public relations and promotional efforts should always be consistent with the content on your site and be targeted specifically to your target audience.

ates to drive visitor traffic, according to the magazine's survey. For instance, 43.2 percent of web merchants who took part in the survey indicated that their affiliate marketing program is at least four years old, compared with 23.2 percent who said they've had a program in place for two to three years, and 10.5 percent with programs only about a year old.

For you, getting a share is simple. You put a few links on your site to any of the thousands of e-tailers or online firms that offer commissions to affiliates, and as surfers click from your site into your affiliated site, you earn money. Basically, you are getting paid for leads, which a practice as old as selling and one that makes sense for everyone involved.

GOOGLE ADSENSE MAKES SENSE

Recently, one of the more significant changes in affiliate marketing has been the emergence of Google's AdSense (google.com/adsense). AdSense allows anyone who publishes online content to display text-based Google AdWords with a simple cut-and-paste format and receive a share of the pay-per-click payment. AdSense ads are similar to the AdWords ads you

TIP

Yahoo also has its own advertising option for small publishers called Yahoo Publisher Network (publisher.yahoo.com). As with Google's service, Yahoo's self-serve product displays text ads deemed relevant to the content of specific web pages. Advertisers pay only when a reader clicks on their ad.

see on the right side of the page at Google.

There are many pluses to using AdSense. Proponents say AdSense is simple and free to join, you do not have to use different codes for various affiliate programs, and you can concentrate on providing good content, because Google does the work of finding the best ads for your pages from 100,000 AdWords advertisers.

The payment you receive per click depends on how much advertisers are paying per click to advertise using Google's AdWords service. Advertisers can pay as little as 5 cents per click or as much as $10 or $12 in profitable niches, perhaps even more. You earn a share of that.

A key reason for the success of AdSense is its revenue model: It is a cost-per-click model versus a cost-per-action or cost-per-sale model. In other words, for affiliates to get paid, visitors to a site just have to complete their click instead of having to complete a transaction.

E-MAIL MARKETING

For many online business owners, e-mail is a great tool for building traffic because it gets results: Customized e-mail can generate response rates upwards of 6 percent—sometimes as high as 30 percent.

Many online startups use e-mail to create a relationship with their current customers or prospects. A great way to start an e-mail list is to ask your visitors or customers to sign up and to permit your company to send messages to them.

What should be included in the content of an e-mail message? Many boutique owners send offers, coupon specials, and product updates to their own list of customers and site visitors who have given them permission to contact them. Personalizing the subject line and the message also may increase your results.

While it is a big commitment in time, publishing a monthly e-mail newsletter is one of the very best ways to keep in touch with your customers, generate trust, develop brand awareness, and build future business. E-letters can contain industry news, in addition to news about new products or special offers you may want to promote. In general, it helps you collect e-mail addresses from those who visit your site and make a purchase—or are not yet ready to make a purchase. Ask for an e-mail address and first name so that you can personalize the newsletter.

The best way to get people to respond to e-mail, however, is to follow the law. In 2004, Controlling the Assault of Non-Solicited Pornography and Marketing Act (the CAN-SPAM Act of 2003) was signed into law. The law requires commercial e-mail messages to be labeled and to include opt-out instructions and the sender's physical address. It also prohibits the use of deceptive subject lines and false headers.

A good way to get folks to opt-in to your e-mail list—which, of course, they will also have the option of opting out of—is to offer a free monthly e-mail newsletter.

Content is wide open, but effective newsletters usually mix news about trends in your field with tips and updates on sales or special pricing. Whatever you do, keep it short; probably 600 words is the maximum length. Another key: Include hyperlinks so that interested readers can,

CAN-SPAM UPDATES

On July 7, 2008, the FTC put into effect new rule provisions surrounding CAN-SPAM. In general, the new rule provisions of the CAN-SPAM Act include changes to the unsubscribe requirements, clarification to the definition of "sender," and the permission to use a valid post office box address to fulfill the CAN-SPAM Act's requirement for a physical address to be displayed in the e-mail. Additionally, the FTC provided clarity to the types of entities that are obligated to comply with CAN-SPAM, including non-profits and individuals.

For more information on the CAN-SPAM Act and the new provisions—as well as advice on how to minimize the risks of e-mail marketing, check out a whitepaper titled "Email Marketing CAN-SPAM Compliance" from e-mail software and services provider ExactTarget at email.exacttarget.com/ETWeb/canspam.aspx. The whitepaper addresses the practical and legal aspects of the CAN-SPAM Act and provides advice on how to minimize the risks of e-mail marketing.

with a single mouse click, go directly to your site and find out more about a topic of interest.

Keep in mind that there are targeted e-mail lists that consist of people who have agreed to receive commercial e-mail messages that you can rent. In general, these lists cost $40 to $400 per thousand, or 4 to 40 cents per name.

One good idea is to do a smaller e-mail test first to determine the quality of the list. You will probably want to find an e-mail list broker to help you with this project. You could save money, your sanity, and get experienced help for no additional cost.

Because maintaining an e-mail list can be time-consuming, a solution to common mailing hassles is to use an e-mail service provider. When choosing an ESP, the ESP should be an expert on all things e-mail and should share this information proactively to improve the effectiveness of your e-mail. It should also understand and be able to advise you on legal issues from a best-practice perspective in all the markets where you send e-mail messages—including other countries. The provider should offer support when needed by you, not when it is convenient for it, and it should be able to help you imple-

TIP

Want to learn more about CAN-SPAM and how it affects business e-mailers? Check out the following link at the Federal Trade Commission's website: ftc. gov/bcp/edu/pubs/business/ ecommerce/bus61.shtm.

ment advanced tools such as dynamic content and web analytics into your e-mail campaigns. Finally, it should offer reports regularly that show how a particular campaign is performing for you.

Three good choices for online business owners just starting out include: Constant Contact (constantcontact.com), ExactTarget (exacttarget.com), and Topica (topica.com). These services maintain mailing lists and on your schedule send out the mailings you provide.

A lot of the grunt work involved in e-mailings is handled by these services, which leaves you free to focus on the fun part: your message. Keep it simple, keep it sharp, and always use e-mail to drive traffic to your site. Do not make the big mistake of trying to cram your website's entire message into every e-mail. Nobody has the patience for that. E-mail should stick to headline news, with the full story residing on your website.

There is no reason to guess at whether or not your list is succeeding. Just track site traffic for a few days before a mailing and a few days afterward. Effective e-mail ought to produce a sharp upward spike in

TIP

Want to use e-mail in a whole new way? Then buy a text ad in an e-mail newsletter—not yours, but someone else's. Some of the best buys are small text ads in e-mail newsletters targeted at audiences likely to be interested in your products or services. Or consider exchanging e-mail newsletter ads with complementary businesses to reach new audiences. Just be sure that your partners are careful where they get their mailing list or you could be in trouble with the CAN-SPAM Act.

visitors. How big a spike hinges on your usual traffic, the size of your list, and your personal goals. A good target, though, is the 6 percent response rate.

If you do not see an increase in traffic, take a hard look at what you are mailing. Is it succinct? Focused? Does it encourage readers to click through for more information? If not, odds are you need to hone your message to encourage recipients to click through.

Another possible reason for less-than-desirable results is that your mailing list is bad. Send a vegan mailing to a list of self-proclaimed steak lovers, and you are knocking on the wrong door. The best way to build a targeted mailing list is to make it simple for site visitors to sign up to receive your e-mails. By doing that, they show they are interested enough in your message to indicate they want to hear more from you. Those are the folks who should be stimulated by your e-mail newsletter to click through for more info, at least sometimes. Keep working on both your newsletter and your list, and it will happen for you, too.

The internet also offers thousands of very targeted e-mail based discussion lists, online forums, blogs, and Usenet newsgroups made up of people with very specialized interests. Use Google Groups to find appropriate sources (groups.google.com). Do not bother with newsgroups that consist of pure spam. Instead, find groups where a serious dialog is taking place. Also, be sure not to use aggressive marketing or overtly plug your online business. Add to the discussion in a helpful way and let the signature at the end of your e-mail message do your marketing for you. People will gradually get to know and trust you, visit your site, and do business with you.

TRADITIONAL MEDIA

For some online startups, traditional media—used in conjunction with e-mail, search, and other digital marketing tools—is very effective. For example, try promoting your online business through display or classified ads you purchase in trade journals, newspapers, and the Yellow Pages, among other venues. But be sure to prominently display your URL in any advertising. In fact, view your website as an information adjunct to the ad. Use a two-step approach: First, capture readers' attention with the ad, and second, refer them to a URL where they can obtain more information and perhaps place an order.

Also look carefully at small display or classified ads in the back of narrowly targeted magazines or trade periodicals. Sometimes these ads are more targeted, more effective, and less expensive than online advertising.

In addition, consider other traditional media to drive people to your site: direct mail, classifieds, and postcards, among other ad vehicles. TV can be used to promote websites, especially in a local market. Additionally, make sure to take advantage of any public relations opportunities. Send press releases to trade reporters or local news organizations. Many of these organizations love to write about small, successful businesses, especially those selling interesting items. But there is more to it then just randomly calling reporters in your industry. Here are some tips for getting press for your online business.

- **Do your homework.** Target television programs, cable programs, newspapers, and trade magazines, among other media vehicles, that fit with your products or services.

- **Create a professional-looking press kit.** Approach this as you would applying for a job. Create a cover letter addressed to a person. Find this person on the masthead of the magazine or the credits of a TV show. Add a few pictures of your merchandise—or yourself, if you are selling a service—a bio page, and your contact information, and you've got the basics. For a really professional looking press kit, you may have to use a freelancer. Note: Because many people today prefer an e-mail press kit, think about turning your press kit into a PDF document and sending it—with a cover letter—via e-mail.

- **Tell a story.** This is a key task. How do you create a compelling narrative? By sharing a little bit about yourself on your bio page. What is your design inspiration? Why did you start an online business? Write a quick one or two lines about your marketing philosophy or about the merchandise you sell.

- **Be timely.** Remember that TV shows and magazines work about three months in advance of airing or print. Newspapers (do not forget local publications) have a shorter lead time, with one exception: Do not submit something that talks about holiday gift guides in November, as they have set these issues months before.

- **Be patient.** Take the time to evolve your business image and learn to edit your descriptions. Learn about the industry and discover your niche. Do not worry if you are not in the black yet. It takes time to grow a healthy business. Keep your goals realistic while still having the stretch goal of world domination.

- **Be professional.** Respond in a timely manner to queries about your shop, keep the casual chatter with reporters to a minimum, and remember, relationships are everything.

SOCIAL MEDIA MARKETING AND ONLINE BUSINESSES

TIP

Do you include your URL on your stationery, cards, and other literature? This no-brainer is sometimes overlooked. Make sure that all reprints of cards, stationery, brochures, and literature contain your company's URL. And see that your printer gets the URL syntax correct. In print, include only the domain.com portion.

Internet marketing has given birth to social media marketing, and it would be wise for online startups to take notice. What is social media marketing?

Basically, it is a form of internet marketing that seeks to achieve branding and marketing communication goals through participation in various social media networks such as MySpace (myspace.com), Facebook (facebook.com), and YouTube (youtube.com), and through social web applications, such as reddit (reddit.com), Digg (digg.com), Stumbleupon (stumbleupon.com), Flickr (flickr.com), iLike (ilike.com), Wikipedia (wikipedia.org), Squidoo (squidoo.com), and Twitter (twitter.com). It also includes working within 3D virtual worlds, such as Second Life (secondlife.com), ActiveWorlds (activeworlds.com), Moove (moove.com), and There.com (there.com).

Social media marketing is part of the umbrella term "Web 2.0." This is a trend in web technology and web design where a second generation of web-based communities and hosted services such as social-networking sites, wikis, blogs, and "folksonomies" facilitate creativity, collaboration, and sharing among users. The central theme of these sites is user-generated content with the social aspects of allowing users to set up social communities, invite friends and share common interests. The communities or social sites can also become areas where a company can generate revenue through targeted advertising. Because these areas offer a very impassioned group of people interested in specific things, advertisers are interested in them. Social media marketing also refers to the blogs, wikis, podcasts, or RSS feeds that online business owners use on their websites or in other communications with customers and suppliers.

In general, the goals of each social media marketing program or campaign differ for every business or organization, but most involve some form of building an idea or brand awareness, increasing visibility, and encouraging brand feedback and dialogue, in addition to selling a product or service.

FUNDAMENTAL SOCIAL MEDIA STEPS

Here are some fundamental steps to take with social media:

- Declare who you are to the online community. If not, nobody will know you and most people do not like associating with total strangers. A great way to do this is to create an "About Us" page and list your achievements and skills.

- Spend an hour every week developing your online social network in MySpace or Facebook. Invite a few of these new friends to write blog articles at your site about your products or services.

- Install free blog software and start publishing at least one article.

- Write articles on your site and blog and provide an action button for each article in your site. The action button takes users to the submission page of the bookmarking sites.

- Provide a forum at your site for users to discuss your products and services. Do not delete negative comments, because they provide insights into the improvements needed to serve your visitors better. However, censor hateful and meaningless content. Then register your forum at Board Tracker (boardtracker.com), a forum search engine. Allow users to review and rate your products. This will help you in inventory management, because you may want to discontinue low-rated products.

- Provide RSS feeds for your new products, blogs, and forum postings, among other items. An RSS feed provides teasers of your contents. Users will use RSS readers to scan your teasers and visit your site for more information if the teasers draw their attentions.

- Publish all your feeds at FeedBurner (feedburner.com). FeedBurner provides media distribution and audience engagement services for RSS feeds. It also provides an advertising network for your feeds. If you have quality contents, you will be able to utilize it by using Feedburner services.

- Provide embedded links to your posted videos in your site. This will save your bandwidth and storage space because the videos reside in the video sharing sites.

- Create how-to or new product videos and post these videos in social video sharing sites such as YouTube and Google video. Provide a few start and end frames in these videos to introduce your site with your site URL. Post these videos using titles, teasing descriptions, and appropriate tags to make them discoverable.

- Besides videos, use social photo sharing sites to share pictures related to contents in your site. Use the same title, description and tag techniques discussed earlier for social video sites.

- Provide a "Send to Friend" feature for all products and services you offer. This feature is a link that sends the article, product description, and other information to a recipient by e-mail. For starters, Yahoo provides a service called Yahoo! Action Buttons (publisher.yahoo.com/social_media_tools) that adds links to your website for users to share, save, and blog about your website. Essentially, they make the Yahoo action buttons use Delicious.com (delicious.com) for social bookmarking, and Yahoo! Search Blog (ysearchblog.com) for blogging. It also has a print feature.

Social media marketing is here to stay and it brings profound changes to web surfers' experiences. It is the right time to implement features that will make your site social media friendly.

STICK IT TO ME

Creating a site that is "sticky" is the dream that keeps website builders going. When your site is sticky, visitors hang around. That means they are reading and buying—and you can bet that every minute a surfer sticks to your site translates into greater brand awareness for you. The stickiest sites have good content that gives users reasons to linger, to absorb more of what you are offering. In addition, sticky sites are easy to navigate.

If you want to sell more products or services to customers who arrive at your website, you need to offer a selection of products or services that people will fall in love with. But in addition to that, the "usability" experience your visitors have while shopping on your website is crucial. Remember, because you are not there in person to guide them through

THE TRUE COST OF FREE SERVICES

Before signing up with any social networking sites, take a close look. What stage is the service in? If it is in alpha, it might change considerably when (and if) it reaches its final form. How much traffic does it get? Alexa (alexa.com) can give you statistics. Finally, what do you receive for contributing free content?

Be careful not to underestimate the true cost of free services. If you sign up for too many and spread yourself too thin, you are losing time you could devote to other aspects of your business. Look at the traffic logs provided by your website's ISP, or install tracking software to find out which of these services actually refers visitors to your website; StatCounter (statcounter.com) and ShinyStat (shinystat.com) offer free versions, as do many others.

the sale, your site has to do that for you. Make sure to remove any barriers your customers might have in getting around your site, finding what they want, and checking out.

Your online business does not have to have all of the following functions, but usability studies show that these features increase online sales. Adding even a few of them to your site can help you sell more products and services.

Website Features

- Site map
- FAQ (frequently asked questions)
- Site-search or product-search feature
- Contact form/easily visible e-mail address
- Size chart/other help with choosing the right product size

- Clear website navigation links
- "About" page that introduces the product designer and establishes a relationship with customers
- Wish-list feature
- Refer-a-friend/tell-a-friend feature

Product Images

- Ability to zoom in / click to enlarge images
- More than one view of each product, including close-ups of details
- Images showing all the colors or other options available for a particular style

On-Site Marketing

- Featured item page
- Clearance sale page
- Promotion of best selling items
- Online-only sale
- Targeted gift ideas (for example, stocking stuffer gift ideas, teacher gift ideas, and niece gift ideas)
- Volume discounts (save money when you buy more than one of an item)
- Cross-selling (recommend and link to related products on your site)
- Testimonials/customer reviews
- Gift certificates available

Checkout/Payment (if selling merchandise):

- Accept credit cards

- Accept debit cards
- Accept PayPal
- Accept checks/money orders
- Redeem gift certificates
- Loyalty/repeat customer/club discount or bonus
- First-time buyer discount

Shipping/Delivery (if selling merchandise)

- Option to buy online, then pick up the order from your studio
- Free standard shipping
- Free upgrade to a faster shipping method
- Holiday shipping deadlines calendar

Customer Service

- Personalized e-mail or autoresponder messages (with a customer's name and possibly other personal details inserted)
- Faster order fulfillment option
- Free gift wrap
- E-mail newsletter to keep customers updated on your products, news, events, and specials
- Blog to keep customers updated on your products, news, events, and specials
- Privacy statement
- Assurance of secure online payment

Basically, your website needs to give people the most user-friendly online shopping experience possible, while making them feel completely secure about buying from your site.

TAPPING INTERNATIONAL MARKETS

One of the lures of the web is that once your online business is up, you are open for business around the world 24 hours a day. But do not be too quick to believe the hype at face value. Yes, you are open 24/7, but international sales may prove elusive, and even when you land orders from abroad, you may wonder if they are worth the bother. Shocked?

There are excellent reasons for many online businesses to pursue global business aggressively, but before you let yourself get dazzled by the upside, consider the negatives. When you understand to what extent foreign customers represent their own hassles and you have decided that you still want them, you will find the information you need to grab plenty of international sales. After all, despite the headaches, many overseas buyers purchase many items online.

Here is the root of the problem with selling internationally: Whenever you ship abroad, you enter into a complicated maze of the other country's laws. Assuming you are in the United States, you know Uncle Sam's laws, and you know that one advantage of doing business in the United States is that barriers against interstate commerce are few. For a Nevada e-tailer to ship to California is no more complicated than putting the gizmo in a box and dropping it off at the post office. With some exceptions, few e-tailers collect sales tax on interstate sales.

Sell abroad, however, and it is a quick step into a maze of complexities, including customs. Generally, it is up to the buyer (not you) to pay any customs owed, but make sure your buyers know that additional charges—imposed by their home countries and payable directly to them—may be owed. You can pick up the forms you will need at any U.S. post office.

Some countries also charge a national sales tax or a value-added tax (around 20 percent on many items in many European countries). Again, as a small foreign retailer, you can pretty safely not worry about collecting these monies, but your buyers may (and probably will) be asked to pay, and they need to understand this is not a charge on your end.

Mailing costs, too, escalate for foreign shipments. Airmail is the best way to go for just about any package, and that gets pricey. A one-pound parcel post shipment to Europe costs more than $10, for instance. Insurance, too, is a must for most shipments abroad, primarily because the more miles a package travels, the bigger chance of damage or loss. Costs are low (insuring a $100 item costs about $2.50 with the U.S. Postal Service), but they still add to the charges you have to pass on to the customer. Add up the many fees—customs, value-added taxes, postage, insurance—and what might initially seem a bargain price to a buyer can easily be nudged into the stratosphere.

Getting authorization on foreign credit cards can also be time-consuming. Although many major U.S. cards are well entrenched abroad (especially American Express and Diner's Club), and validating them for a foreign cardholder is frequently not difficult, this process can be fraught with risks for the merchant, so be careful.

If you are still not discouraged, do one more reality check to make sure international sales make sense for you. Is what you are selling readily available outside your country? Will what you sell ship reasonably easily and at

TIP

It is tempting: Declare that an item is an unsolicited gift, and the recipient often does not have to pay any customs charges. The amount that can be exempted varies from country to country; usually it is $50 to $100. However, do not make that declaration even if a buyer asks (and savvy ones frequently will)—they are asking you to break the law.

a favorable price? Even with the costs of shipping factored in, will buying from you rather than from domestic sellers be a benefit to your customers? If you pass these tests, you are ready to get down to business.

Step One in getting more global business is to make your site as friendly as possible to foreign customers. Does this mean you need to offer the site in multiple languages? For very large companies, yes However, the cost of doing a good translation is steep, and worse, whenever you modify pages—which ought to be regularly—you will need to get the new material translated, too.

Small sites can usually get away with using only English and still prosper abroad. Consider this: Search for homes for sale on Greek islands, and you will find as many sites in English as in Greek. Why English? Because it has emerged as an international language. A merchant in Athens will probably know English because it lets him talk with French, German, Dutch, Turkish and Italian customers. An English-only website will find fluent readers in many nations. But keep the English on your site as simple and as traditional as possible. The latest slang may not have made its way to English speakers in Istanbul or Tokyo.

To make your site more user-friendly for foreign customers,

TIP

When is a foreign customer not a foreign customer? When he or she wants you to ship to a U.S. address (perhaps an Edinburgh father sending a birthday gift to his daughter at a Boston college) or when the customer is an American in the military or diplomatic corps (shipping to their addresses is no different from mailing to a domestic address). Do not judge an e-mail address by its domain. The address may end in "it" (Italy) or "de" (Germany), but it can still be a U.S. order.

put up a page—clearly marked—filled with tips intended especially for them. If you have the budget, get this one page translated into various key languages. (A local college student might do a one-page translation for approximately $20.) Use this space to explain the complexities involved in buying abroad. Cover many of the hassles we just discussed, but rephrase the material so it looks at matters through the buyer's eyes. By all means, include the benefits, too, but do not leave anything out, because the more clear a customer's thinking before pressing the "Buy" button, the more likely he or she is to complete the transaction.

TIP

Want a no-cost translation of your site? Offer a link to PROMT-Online, a free online translation service (translation2.paralink.com). Before putting this up, however, ask friends—or pay an expert—to take a look at the translation. These types of services usually offer excellent translations, but you do not want your site's translation to be the embarrassing exception.

In the meantime, routinely scan your log files for any patterns of international activity. If you notice that, say, Norway is producing a stream of visitors and no orders, this may prompt you to search for ways to coax Norwegians into buying. Try including a daily special "for Norwegian mailing addresses only" or perhaps running a poll directed at Norwegians.

Clues about foreign visitors will also help you select places to advertise your site. While an ad campaign on Yahoo may be beyond your budget, it is entirely realistic to explore, say, ads on Yahoo Sweden. If you notice an increase in visitors (or buyers!) from a specific country, explore the cost of mounting a marketing campaign that explicitly targets them.

At the end of the day, whether you reap substantial foreign orders or not is up to you. If you want them, they can be grabbed, because the promise of the web is true in the sense that it wipes out time zones, borders and other barriers to commerce. That does not mean these transactions are easy—they can be challenging, as you've seen—but for the e-commerce entrepreneur determined to sell globally, there is no better tool than the web.

OH CANADA!

Although Canadians still lag a bit behind U.S. consumers when it comes to online shopping, that is starting to change. According to a June 2006 survey by J.C. Williams Group (jcwg.com) of 1,312 Canadians who had purchased online in the past six months, 32 percent made five or more purchases, and 68 percent made one to four purchases. Canadian e-commerce is growing substantially as well, with total e-commerce sales totaling $32.4 billion ($39.2 billion Cdn) in 2005, up 38.4 percent from 2004.

"U.S. retailers are looking for expansion possibilities internationally, and Canada is a friendly way to test systems and processes in an initial expansion strategy," says Maris Daugherty, senior consultant of multichannel practice at J.C. Williams Group in Chicago. "In addition, U.S. retailers are not too far from home, there is untapped demand in Canada, and many Canadian retailers have not yet included e-commerce among their sales channels."

To design a website that meets the needs of Canadians, use a single e-commerce platform that supports all countries. "The platform should have the ability to be centrally supported with localized content areas and processes defined by country, so the customer can choose their country of preference when they arrive, and it will then be customized by specific cultural options," Daugherty says. "In Canada, that would include language options in French or English, total pricing including sales tax and shipping charges represented in Canadian dollars, and customer service hours that reflect Canadian regions with availability to both English- and French-speaking agents."

STELLAR CUSTOMER SERVICE: DO YOU HAVE WHAT IT TAKES?

The great thing about the internet is that anyone can set up shop. Of course, that means you have to compete with the big guys—and customer service is no exception. "Customers today are very savvy," says Lauren Freedman, president of the e-tailing group inc. (e-tailing.com), an e-commerce consulting firm in Chicago. "They expect best-of-breed customer service everywhere they shop on the web. They do not care if you are smaller."

Each year, Freedman's firm tracks the top 100 e-tailers on 11 criteria relative to customer service and communication. The most successful online e-tailers offer the following:

1. **Toll-free number.** "This is pretty critical today," says Freedman. "If a small business does not offer this now, it should think about it."

2. **Keyword search.** According to Freedman, "People today are used to searching for things online, and they want a seamless search experience on the websites they are considering buying from."

3. **Timely answers to e-mail questions.** "A small e-tailer should probably strive for 48 hours," says Freedman, who adds it is important to personally address customer queries instead of just sending automated responses.

4. **Four or fewer days to receive a package via ground shipping.** "A small e-tailer should try to strive for five business days," says Freedman. "And they should make it very clear—in all their communications with their customers—what their shipping policies are."

5. **Six or fewer clicks to checkout.**

6. **Inventory status.** While real-time status is best, "[Let] your customer know within 24 hours if the product they are ordering is in stock or is not in stock," says Freedman.

7. **Online shipping status.** "[Offer] a link to UPS or FedEx so that they can check their orders on their sites," says Freedman.

8. **Order confirmation in the shopping cart.**

9. An e-mail order confirmation with the order number included.

10. **Recommendations for other products and features during the shopping process.** "This is a standard for the larger merchants, but something that small e-merchants should strive for," says Freedman, who adds doing so can help you increase order size.

11. **Clearly displayed customer service hours.** This is especially important if you have limited customer service hours, says Freedman.

CONCLUSION

The following is a list of what customers expect from an online business today. Clip it out and keep it taped to your computer. You should always be thinking about your customers.

1. **Stellar customer service.** Consumers may take advantage of shopping online in order to avoid salespeople, but what if they want to ask a question or change their mind about a selection they made? Does your online business have a telephone number where they can speak to customer service? If so, what hours are they available (be sure to verify time zones)?

2. **Clear information.** Make sure you have clear information on guarantees, secure ordering, lost/damaged shipments, and returns. Consumers want to be sure the purchase is guaranteed and that their purchase price can be refunded if they need to return the items.

3. **Good shipping choices.** If you are selling any type of merchandise, consumers want to know that the online business with whom they are doing business—in addition to their suppliers—ship using insured carriers such as FedEx and UPS and that all shipments are insured for the full value of their contents. Be sure to do this.

4. **Clear images.** If a shopper finds a product that interests them, he wants to make sure he can click its image to make it larger to get a better look. While this is not necessarily a good substitute for seeing the piece in person, it will give him a pretty good idea of what the piece looks like.

5. **Have secure transactions.** Today, most online businesses guarantee that all personal information consumers provide for payment or registration purposes is automatically encrypted by the latest security software. It eliminates the risk of data interception, manipulation, or recipient impersonation by unauthorized parties. Because consumers want this security, make sure you give it to them.

6. **Have a privacy policy.** Most online businesses today that collect any personal data (even an e-mail address) have their privacy policy posted. Consumers review these privacy policies to confirm that their private information will not be sold to other companies, specifically marketing companies or partners with similar products. Make sure you do not do this.

PART II:
55 ONLINE BUSINESSES

ACCESSORIES AND APPAREL SALES

This type of venture can be very lucrative. Before launching this kind of online business, decide what type of apparel and accessories you'd like to sell. Children's? Women's? Men's? And there are even more categories within categories to think about. Will you sell high-end designer fashions? Off-the-rack sales by volume? Will you sell sportswear? Prom attire? Plus sizes? Should you run the gamut?

In this type of business, specialization is a plus. In fact, specialization, or finding your niche in this business, is crucial to your success. In many cases, all it takes is a little common sense. While there are many apparel and accessory stores on the web today, there is always room for more—especially the right kind of apparel store.

What are some of the talents or skills you should possess before going full steam ahead with this type of business? A passion for fashion, knowledge of the fashion industry, plenty of competitive research, and due diligence, to name a few.

Where will you get your merchandise? Most e-tailers work with wholesalers or distributors who offer lower price merchandise and sell it in bulk.

Before launching this business, understand that there are some challenges to it. The biggest hurdle is the customers' demand to simulate on the internet the "see, feel and touch" experience they get when buying clothes in a brick-and-mortar store. When buying clothes, customers want to know if the selected item fits them well and whether they would look good in those clothes. First, you have to provide as much information on the clothes as possible. Given the overwhelming concern with fit and correct sizing, present sizing information to help consumers understand the products better. Use various metrics to measure the size of the clothes, even the length and width, as well as the kind and quality of fabric.

The quality of the product's photos must also be ensured. While the varying colors of computer screens and monitors are beyond the control of an e-tailer, small businesses can benefit by spending more resources in getting better-quality pictures of their products up on their sites. You can also use rich media tools, which are getting less expensive each day.

You'll also need to address the consumer's concerns with having to return garments. Small businesses do not have the wide retail channel enjoyed by top retailers such as Gap.com where customers can return purchases bought online to the nearest Gap retail store. Instead, small businesses can make sure that clear and detailed instructions on how to return purchased items are provided on the site. The cardinal rule to be followed is to make the process for returning the product as easy as the process for buying them. One strategy may be to offer guarantees to customers for a full 30 days to return products for refund, exchange, or store credit.

To build this business, market your online store all over the place. Price your merchandise accordingly, and start off with plenty of sales and specials such as buy-one-get-one-free, or save 35 percent on accessories if you buy a gown. Another good strategy is to add product reviews and other information on your site along with the clothes. This content will position you as an authority on the subject and offer your customers or visitors a reason to keep coming back to the site to browse or buy. Other good tools for apparel and accessory sales are shopping comparison sites and using social media marketing techniques. In fact, studies show that heavy social networkers visit retail sites.

Finally, remember that repeat business is the key to your success, so ask customers what they want and deliver it to them; provide excellent customer service; have a fair return policy; and start an e-mail newsletter for your customers. This could provide bits of fashion advice while providing plenty of promotion for your shop. Your goal should be to build trust with your visitors by delivering great content and information. That helps you build consistent traffic and bring buyers to your online store.

SKILLS NEEDED

You'll need a passion for fashion, knowledge of the fashion industry, the ability to compile competitive research, and great customer service skills.

THINGS TO CONSIDER

In this type of business, specialization is a plus. In fact, specialization, or finding your niche in this business, is crucial to your success. Also, make sure you provide as much information on the clothes as possible, and make the quality of the product's photos excellent. Finally, address the consumer's concerns with having to return garments, such as offering a full 30-day guarantee to customers to return products for refund, exchange, or store credit.

WEB RESOURCES

Alloy (alloy.com), teen-oriented apparel and accessory boutique
Apparel showroom (apparelshowroom.com), wholesale clothing site
Bluefly (bluefly.com), a leading online apparel store
eLuxury.com (eluxury.com), an online fashion retailer offering designer
apparel and accessories, beauty and children's collections
Threadless (threadless.com), a provider of artsy t-shirts

2 AD NETWORK

A d networks organize the sale of web-based ads and find high-traffic sites—or targeted sites—on which to place the banner ads or hyper links. They are a leading online advertising method today.

In some ways, they are just like traditional advertising agencies in that they find the best places to place ads. However, unlike traditional agencies, they are not seeking advertising space on television, radio, or in print; instead, they are seeking out websites that attract the target demographic of their clients.

The advertising network serves advertisements from its ad server, which responds to a site once a page is called. A snippet of code is called from the ad server that represents the advertising banner. You make money by getting a percentage of advertising dollars that you retain during each campaign.

You can launch an online network that pushes ads to general websites, thereby reaching a mass audience, or you can design a niche-oriented network—also known as a vertical network—that targets ads from specific types of merchants or advertisers to specific websites. You also can start even more sophisticated networks that offer geo-targeted ads or ads based on behavioral targeting. These types of networks are a bit more sophisticated—and a bit more expensive—to start. For $5,000, it's probably best to start with a mass-marketed ad network.

Before launching this business, it is important to have a deep knowledge of online advertising techniques. Also, if you want to offer banner ad design services, knowledge of graphic design would be beneficial, so you do not have to outsource the ad design.

To market this type of business, why not develop a comprehensive affiliate/associate program? This would not only increase awareness of your ad network, it would also send referral business to your site. You should also get links from online directories, use search engine optimization and search engine marketing techniques, participate in newsgroups and discussion forums related to online advertising or the industry you are targeting, or even launch your own online advertising campaign on sites frequented by your target market.

SKILLS NEEDED

Without a doubt, to be successful in this business, you must have knowledge of online advertising techniques. What's more, if you decide to offer banner ad and design services, knowledge of graphic design would be a plus. Of course, it's important to have excellent written communication skills as well as superior customer service and marketing skills.

THINGS TO CONSIDER

The software you choose for this business will make or break it—so choose wisely. Be prepared to deal with things such as excess capacity ad space by using such strategies as last-minute volume discounts. Always ask to get paid up front for an advertising campaign. Also, understand that you can launch an online network that pushes ads to general websites, a niche-oriented network, or an even more sophisticated network that offers geo-targeted ads or ads to specific web pages based on behavioral targeting. These types of networks are more complex and they are expensive to start up. To stay within a limited budget, it's probably best to start with the mass-marketed ad network.

WEB RESOURCES

Advertising.com (advertising.com), operator of the largest display advertising network in the U.S.

Burst Media (burstmedia.com), an online media and technology company and online advertising network

Outside Hub (outsidehub.com), a leading online ad network for the outdoor enthusiast market

Travel Ad Network (traveladnetwork.com), a vertical internet ad network that sells ads on top-tier travel websites

ART PRINT SALES

Selling art prints online can be a very lucrative business. You can develop a website that exclusively sells art prints, and the site can be indexed by print theme, artist, or any categories you like. You can also focus on a particular niche and carry art prints from a specific time period or with a similar theme

You can either sell merchandise purchased from wholesalers or art dealers, or artists from around the world can submit pictures of their prints to be posted and subsequently sold. After a print is sold, the wholesaler, dealer, or artist would ship it to the purchaser and receive a percentage of the sales value—which means you do not have to maintain inventory. As a result, this type of cyberventure is relatively easy to establish.

Ideally, marketing efforts should be aimed at individuals and organizations that routinely purchase art prints, such as decorators, corporations, and property developers. Another point: Since you would be selling graphic items, make sure your site is graphically pleasing and easy to navigate.

What type of marketing would make the most sense here? A subscriber e-mail newsletter perhaps, which offers biweekly or monthly updates of new art works being posted. Of course, you should also be sure to use additional online marketing techniques such as search engine optimization, search engine marketing, and other online advertising.

SKILLS NEEDED

You'll need an understanding of art and the art world, including what makes an interesting or pleasing art graphic, the ability to compile competitive research, and great customer service skills.

THINGS TO CONSIDER

In this type of business, make sure your site is as pleasing to the eye as possible. Also, make sure you organize your merchandise and enable people to search through the site by different categories. You may want to focus on a niche, such as selling prints from a specific time period or with a specific theme.

WEB RESOURCES

Art.com (art.com), leading online seller of posters, prints, and framed art

Artprints.com (artprints.com), online seller fine art prints, posters, canvas transfers, and limited editions from thousands of famous artists

Imagekind (imagekind.com), community for creating, buying, and selling high-end framed artwork

Lieberman's Gallery (liebermans.net), oldest and largest one-stop, wholesale consolidator of prints and posters

AUCTION SITE

4

As almost anyone who has ever been online knows, eBay has taken the internet by storm. It is the most successful auction site on the web and is a great example of how you can capitalize on a concept that has never been developed online.

The online auction business model is one in which participants bid for products and services over the internet. Like most auction companies, eBay does not actually sell goods that it owns itself. It merely facilitates the process of listing and displaying goods, bidding on items, and paying for them. It acts as a marketplace for individuals and businesses that use the site to auction off goods and services.

Before even thinking about launching an online auction site, understand that it will be very hard to try to compete with a site that large and respected. However, that does not mean you can't create an auction site and achieve success.

If you want to build a successful auction website, begin by creating your site on a specific, well-defined niche and starting a small auction that caters only to that niche. Once your site becomes successful, you can expand into other areas. For example, consider a site that is focused on baseball cards and collecting. You could create an entire site dedicated to providing information on the cards and discussion groups among other baseball card collectors and enthusiasts. Then, you would use the search engines (Google and MSN, as two examples) to attract people searching for this topic. As your site gains popularity, you can think about offering more categories.

After setting up your site, you will need to use special software program that places items up for auction on your website. The functionality of buying and selling in an auction format is made possible through this auction software, which regulates the various processes involved. When people place bids, this software keeps track of the bids, closes the auction, and notifies the seller and successful bidder. As with eBay and other auction sites, the bidder and the seller arrange for shipping of the item privately. You make money by getting a commission from the sale of each item or the fee charged to submit an item in addition to advertising revenue, if you decide to sell advertising on your site. Some auction sites also charge a membership fee for access to selling on the site.

Besides search engine optimization, you will also want to promote the site auction item through search engine marketing, creating a link strategy, and traditional online advertising.

SKILLS NEEDED

An in-depth understanding of how online auctions work and a strong familiarity with online auction software are required. You'll need contacts who have items available that you can sell on your site. You'll also need great written communication skills, along with excellent marketing and customer service skills. Good website design is also a plus, especially in terms of site navigation, because you'll want to make the site as easy as possible for people to browse. For example, you'll want to include as many categories as possible so it will be easy for people to find exactly what they are seeking.

THINGS TO CONSIDER

Before launching an online auction site, make sure you have found the right niche; in other words, don't try to compete with eBay. Also, be sure to develop great back-end systems that ensure that you are paid your fee or commission.

WEB RESOURCES

Auction.com (auction.com), an online auction site with a robust search feature on its site, making it easy for visitors to search categories

Etsy (etsy.com), an online auction marketplace for buying and selling all things handmade.

eBay (ebay.com) the granddaddy of all auction sites

Public Surplus (publicsurplus.com), a leading online government surplus auction

5 AUDIO EQUIPMENT SALES

Another very hot business opportunity right now is selling audio equipment online. Many successful web businesses are finding riches selling such audio equipment as wireless microphones, amplifiers, mixers, headphones and more. Some also expand their businesses to musical instruments, home theater systems, speakers, car audio equipment, and recording equipment. Or you can specialize and sell a niche product, such as only wireless microphones or amplifiers. To sell this type of merchandise, online retailers can work with audio equipment manufacturers, wholesalers, and suppliers.

Note: Because many of these manufacturers are based in mainland China or Hong Kong, knowing both the Chinese language and their customs is a plus if you plan on working directly with suppliers. Of course, many of these companies' employees speak English, but having that knowledge can help in relationship building.

You may want to target consumers, professional musicians, or recording studios, churches, and schools, but keep in mind that focusing on the bigger sales will probably help you make more money more quickly. When it comes to marketing, use traditional internet marketing techniques, comparison-shopping sites and e-mail marketing.

Because pricing is very important in this space, keep track of what your competition is charging and do the same or better. You also will want to work with a sales and customer service staff that is very knowledgeable in audio, music, sound engineering and troubleshooting. You may even want to hire staff to install or service systems.

SKILLS NEEDED

You'll need an understanding of the audio world, the ability to compile competitive research, and great customer service skills. Knowledge of Chinese is a plus.

THINGS TO CONSIDER

In this type of business, pricing is very important, so make sure you are constantly aware of what your competition is charging for its merchandise. It's also important for you and your customer service staff to have an in-depth knowledge of the merchandise you are selling, so they are able to help with any questions that may come up—and questions will come up.

WEB RESOURCES

Audiogear.com (audiogear.com), an online seller of wireless microphones, amplifiers, mixers, headphones and more

BestBuy Audio (bestbuyaudio.com), a online provider of car audio, home audio and dj equipment with discount pricing on audio equipment

Headsets.com (headsets.com), a leading provider of headsets online

RF Amplifiers (rfamplifiers.com), a provider of radio frequency amplifiers

6 ▶ AUTOMOTIVE PARTS SALES/DIRECTORY

Selling automotive replacement parts for rare, antique, and sports cars can make you rich. Why? Because the internet offers a logical way to mass market an auto replacement parts business. People from all over the world are looking for these types of parts, and because you are on the internet, you can reach all of these people.

With this type of online business, you have several options. The first is to purchase replacement parts at low prices and resell them for a profit at your website. The second option is to create an internet portal that brings people together who are seeking to buy and sell automotive replacement parts. The latter is the less-costly option to choose. After all, you do not have to deal with buying and selling merchandise, and you do not have to worry about inventory.

To create this type of portal, simply build a basic website and offer tons of information pertaining to automotive replacement parts that can be used by car collectors and enthusiasts worldwide. The site can include a directory of parts manufacturers and distributors, in addition to a classifieds section that enables visitors to post "for sale" and "wanted" notices about automotive parts.

To make the site even more appealing, include content that visitors would find interesting, such as car maintenance tips, online mechanics instruction training, and a chat forum for visitors to swap information.

How could income be made form this type of portal? In several ways: You can sell books and repair manuals on the site (in traditional or e-book form), or you can sell advertising space in the directory in the form of online banner ads.

If, however, you decide to go with the first option—sell auto parts—you would need to market to car enthusiasts, in addition to body and fender repair shops and mechanics.

In each example, you will also want to engage in traditional interactive marketing, including search engine marketing and/or optimization, online display ads on targeted sites, and a comprehensive link strategy.

SKILLS NEEDED

An understanding of the automotive world—a must if you are selling rare or antique car parts—excellent marketing skills, and excellent customer service skills as well. If you are creating an online portal with directory listings and content, good writing and editing skills are a plus.

THINGS TO CONSIDER

It's very important for you—and your customer service staff—to have an in-depth knowledge of the merchandise you are selling and be able to deal with any questions that come up—and questions *will* come up.

WEB RESOURCES

A1 Classic Car Parts Finder (classiccarpartsfinder.com), a premier locator of rare auto and truck parts and restorable and parts cars and trucks

Auto Parts Warehouse (autopartswarehouse.com), a leading provider of high-quality parts sold at low prices

AutopartsGiant.com (autopartsgiant.com), a fast growing company that sells auto parts through a comprehensive online parts catalog

Vintage Auto Parts (vapinc.com), a leader in the antique car parts industry

7 BABY PRODUCTS

Oh, baby! Starting a business that focuses on anything baby-related is hot right now. Besides the fact that there is a baby boom going on in our society today, more and more exhausted new parents are turning to the internet so they can shop from the comfort of their own homes—and while their babies are sleeping. There are hundreds of types of products you can sell, from baby furniture to feeding products to clothing and everything in between. You can focus on one area or all areas. If you are focusing on one area, try to find a niche, such as "eco-friendly baby furniture" or "just pacifiers," "high-end baby furniture," or "products for twins." You also may want to include or even focus on pregnancy-related products, which will allow you to focus on two markets (before and after) and, it is hoped, get repeat visitors.

Either way, make sure your pricing is competitive (there are many online stores that sell baby stuff today) and make sure your site is organized by category and easy to navigate.

You will most likely be selling merchandise that you purchased wholesale. As a result, make sure you do your research and determine the best pricing. Because new parents are looking for information, make sure your site offers tons of it, either from the manufacturers or customer reviews. In fact, it may be a good idea to make the customer reviews prominent, because new parents love to share advice with each other.

This concept may also help drive your marketing plans; perhaps start a chat room on your site to get folks to start a dialogue on your site and keep them coming back for more. Or advertise in new parent-oriented chat rooms online. You also will want to offer an online newsletter to regular customers and advertise heavily through search engine optimization and search engine marketing.

SKILLS NEEDED

An in-depth understanding of baby products, as well as an understanding of the types of products that new parents need and want. Excellent marketing skills and excellent customer service skills are also musts as well.

THINGS TO CONSIDER

In this type of business, it's very important for you to find your niche. There are thousands of baby products stores out there today—both online and offline—so it's best to sell something unique. Also, keep in mind that while new parents may be the majority of the people buying on your site, in many cases grandparents or other relatives as well as friends may be your customers, so make sure to appeal to them as well.

WEB RESOURCES

BabyAge.com (babyage.com), the premiere online retailer of pregnancy, infant and juvenile products

Baby Basket.com (babybasket.com), an online designer and creator of distinctive gift baskets for new babies, new moms, new dads, and big brothers and sisters

GreatBaby Products (greatbabyproducts.com), a leading online retailer of baby products

YourBabyStroller (yourbabystroller.com), a leading online provider of baby strollers

8 BOOKSTORE

Online bookstores are one of the most widely accepted forms of online businesses. Since the business leader in the category happens to be the leader online as well—we are talking Amazon.com here—you may want to stay away from the "all-in-one" online bookstore. Instead, take a more targeted approach and start an online bookstore that specializes in a particular type of book. Not only will this distinguish you from online stars such as Amazon.com and BarnesandNoble.com, but it will also allow you to use highly targeted traffic-building techniques.

Setting up an online bookstore gives you some advantages with distributors compared to other online business opportunities. Why? Because typically, book distributors grant longer terms of credit than other distributors or wholesalers. This is great, because books can sit in your inventory for extended periods of time. After all, you do not want to pay for stock that has not yet turned a profit for your online business.

If you do indeed decide to open up a specialized online bookstore, be sure you are knowledgeable on the particular subject of the books you will be selling. You should also understand what your target market's needs are. You will have to know the retail book business thoroughly, including how to handle returns (you will probably have a lot of them; it is just the nature of the beast) and remainders, among other considerations that are particular to retail.

You will also need a very good understanding of deliveries, shipping, and order fulfillment in general. A common issue both large and small online bookstores face is an efficient delivery service. If you tell your clients that your products will be shipped within a 24-hour period, make sure to follow through with this.

To offer the best possible shipping method for your customers, research the service and prices offered by the major carriers (USPS, UPS, FedEx, DHL) so that you know what is right for your business—and for your customers.

Finally, keeping the most current inventory information on your website is crucial. In fact, your website should be database-driven. For example, many successful online bookstores offer value-added information for each selection listed on their site. This information could be anything from customer reviews to biographies to chapter excerpts. Think about what Amazon.com, for example, does for its listings. All of this information will enhance your listings and will entice visitors to buy—or at least come back for more.

As is the case with all online businesses, marketing is extremely important in this space. Why not develop a comprehensive affiliate marketing program, which will not only send referrals to your bookstore, but also increase the overall awareness of your site?

You could also launch a banner advertising campaign on websites frequented by your target market. The banner ads can send high volumes of traffic to your site. And to make it even more attractive, why not add a coupon to the banner to entice folks to come to the site? This can also be used as a tracking mechanism; you test an online banner-ad campaign with a coupon and see how many people link to your site by clicking on the coupon link. Nifty idea, huh? You will also want to use search engine marketing and optimization techniques, an e-mail and/or viral marketing program, and a comprehensive link strategy; you might even develop a loyalty program for frequent shoppers.

SKILLS NEEDED

You'll need an in-depth understanding of the book business, including the supply chain, how to handle returns, remainders, and so on. If you're focusing on a specific niche of books, you'll also need to be an expert in that particular field. You'll also need strong online marketing skills—especially if you plan on competing with Amazon.com—as well as excellent communication and customer service skills. You'll also want to have an in-depth knowledge of delivery and fulfillment issues.

THINGS TO CONSIDER:

Before launching this business, investigate all of the possible shipping options. For example, get to know your local postmaster, and read all the literature available on FedEx and UPS. You'll want to offer your customers the best delivery options possible, especially because today, most people expect to receive their book packages from online merchants on time and in good condition, thanks to Amazon.com!

WEB RESOURCES

Alibris (alibris.com), the premier marketplace for sellers of new, used, and out-of-print books, music items, and movies

Amazon.com (amazon.com), the world's leading online bookstore

American Book Company (americanbookco.com), a wholesale distributor of promotional, closeout, remainder, and bargain priced books

Buteo Books (buteobooks.com), a specialty online bookstore with one of the largest selections of bird books in the world

CAR RESEARCH SERVICE

You can provide visitors with access to and information about new and pre-owned automobiles and related products and services through an online car research service.

This type of site allows consumers to research, price, order, purchase, insure, and finance a vehicle online via an intuitive website that offers product information for nearly every make, model, and style of automobile available in the United States. You can also offer vehicle reviews, ratings, safety features, and specifications. Customers may even be able to simultaneously compare the specifications of competing vehicles, or search for available manufacturer rebates and incentives on any new vehicle. In most cases, much of this data comes from other sources around the internet, such as the Kelly Blue Book, which provides new car prices, and used car values or from the manufacturers themselves.

Good online car research sites also offer photo galleries, videos, and unbiased editorial content. Some sites also offer buying guides written by staffers to help visitors make informed purchases.

Basically, this type of site works like a classified ad service. Your customers will purchase cars through car dealers that pay you to list their cars, and a visitor will type out their zip code and select a car from a local dealer. As a result, to be successful with this service, you have to form relationships with dealers, which can be difficult—but can be done.

Besides getting a fee for listing cars, you can sell advertising on your site. You can also charge a membership fee and give members things such as a weekly e-mail with the newest car listings or interesting car research. In terms of marketing, search engine optimization and marketing is very important in this business; start there first.

SKILLS NEEDED

To be successful in this business, you will need to have expert knowledge in the area of cars and car dealers. You'll also need excellent written communication skills, as well as great customer service and online marketing skills. You'll also need good site design skills, because you'll want to make your site as easy to read as possible, while at the same time making sure the cars you are discussing are attractively showcased.

THINGS TO CONSIDER

People love their cars and usually pay a lot of money for them. Before launching this site, make sure that you have the best available research for your visitors. If not, they won't return. Also, to be successful with this service, you would have to form relationships with dealers, which can be difficult—but can be done.

WEB RESOURCES

Car Finder Service (carfinderservice.com), an online site designed for new or used car buyers that offers information about what to buy and how much to pay

Cars.com (cars.com), a leading online car research service

Carsdirect (carsdirect.com), another leading online car research service

InternetAutoGuide.com (internetautoguide.com), a site that offers new and used car reviews, research, and pricing

CIGAR SALES

Selling cigars online can be a surefire winner. Currently, millions of dollars of cigars are sold online every month in the United States. There are several reasons for this, but a key one is being able to charge low prices for the cigars because of low overhead. Besides the rent and utility costs of owning and running an brick-and-mortar cigar storefront, there is also the need for things such as plasma TVs and leather chairs, which cigar stores often have to buy or rent to create a clubby atmosphere. With an online store, your only focus will be on the sale of high-quality cigars sold at low prices.

There are several ways to go about launching this type of online business. To begin, you can simply purchase cigars from suppliers and resell them on your site at low prices. You will want to work with suppliers that can sell you cigars inexpensively, but make sure you are not getting factory seconds. Make sure you develop good relationships with your suppliers; do your research to find out as much about them as possible before starting to work with them.

You can expand your business by adding cigar accessories, such as cutters and humidors. In many cases, you can get this merchandise from the same suppliers. Do not sell cigarettes. Because cigar smokers think of themselves as a cut above cigarette smokers, selling cigarettes can damage your brand.

Another unique idea is to have a "cigar a day" site, where you feature one product per day. This way, you don't have to maintain massive inventories of every brand and size of cigar available. Instead, you purchase just enough cigars to sell in one day. Large inventories, after all, are expensive and difficult to maintain. By only offering one product each day, you can sell your cigars far cheaper than if you had to spend the time and money to maintain a large inventory.

Either way, shipping is a very important part of this business for a variety of reasons. Most importantly, you have to make sure that you are shipping to people only over the age of 18, the country's legal smoking age. Some sites won't ship to people unless they are at least 21 years old. You will also want to make sure that your cigars are shipped in boxes with packing material on the inside to make sure your orders arrive in top condition.

There is yet another business model you can try: You could develop a website that serves as an online portal to bring cigar manufacturers and distributors together with consumers that purchase cigars.

This type of venture would be very easy to establish, and charging cigar manufacturers and distributors a fee to be listed and featured on the site would generate income. Alternately, income could be earned by retaining a portion of the cigar sales that are created, and listed companies could be posted for free.

To spice up the site and make it more interesting for visitors, you can also add a chat line forum or message board on topics related to cigars, as well as an online poll that lets smokers vote for the all-time best cigars.

Warning: Be careful that your site is not used to bring illegal Cuban cigars into the U.S. or other countries where they are not allowed.

As for marketing, techniques to think about include developing a comprehensive link strategy, participating in newsgroups and e-mail lists that discuss cigars, publishing articles in magazines or e-zines that pertain to cigars, and developing a sponsored listings campaign to bid on appropriate keyword phrases with the leading search engines. You also may want to offer a free catalog and have folks opt-in to be on your e-mail list, which you can use to advertise weekly and one-day specials.

SKILLS NEEDED

Obviously, you will need an in-depth knowledge of cigars and the cigar supply chain to make this business work. It would probably help if you actually smoked cigars, but it is not necessary. You'll also need excellent online marketing and customer-service skills.

THINGS TO CONSIDER

Shipping is a very important part of this business for a variety of reasons. You have to make sure that you are shipping to people only over the age of 18, the country's legal smoking age. Some sites won't ship to people unless they are at least 21 years old. You will also want to make sure that your cigars are shipped in boxes with packing material on the inside to make sure your orders arrive in top condition. Also, make sure that your site does not inadvertently bring Cuban cigars into this country—they are not allowed.

WEB RESOURCES

Cigars International (cigarsinternational.com), a leading provider of cigars, discount cigars, humidors, and cigar accessories

Famous Smoke Shop (famoussmokeshop.com), an easy-to-read, well-designed online cigar shop

JRCigars.com (jrcigars.com), online sellers of machine made and hand-rolled cigars

Thompson Cigar (thompsoncigar.com), an online cigar retailer that offers discounts on cigars, humidors and accessories

11 COLLECTOR'S ITEMS SALES

There are many people who turn to the web for collector's items, such as rare books, memorabilia, and antique items.

As a result, this business is a great one to start online. You can either sell a variety of collector's items, or specialize in a specific type, such as vinyl records or sports memorabilia. A word of caution though: serious hobbyists and collectors of these items know their stuff. Thus, before you venture into this business, make sure that you have an extensive knowledge of rare books, memorabilia, music or other items. Also, make sure you know the value of the items you are selling.

You can sell the items on your site in the traditional fashion or you could also set up all or part of your site as an auction site where people can sell their items. In the latter example, you could take a commission of the final sale or require users to pay up-front to list their item.

The best way to market this type of online business is to develop a link strategy. Music sites, book sites, rarity sites, and collectibles sites are all great places to start link relationships.

You also might want to participate in newsgroups and online discussion forums about the types of memorabilia you are selling. Do not forget about e-mail marketing or participation in a webring, especially since there are many types of webrings that focus on these types of products.

SKILLS NEEDED

An in-depth understanding of collectibles, excellent marketing skills and excellent customer service skills are musts.

THINGS TO CONSIDER

In this type of business, it's very important for you to become an expert at the collectibles you are buying or selling. Those individuals who purchase this type of merchandise are usually passionate, so they will want you to be passionate as well. Many collectibles dealers also may have phony collectibles; if you have a deep understanding of the collectibles you are selling, you will be able to avoid any rip-offs or scams.

WEB RESOURCES

AbeBooks (abebooks.com) an online seller of thousands of rare, collectible, and antique books

Forcecollectors (forcecollectors.com), an online community dedicated to the buying, selling, and trading of Star Wars collectibles, including Star Wars action figures, trading cards, games, toys and memorabilia

Metropolis Comics and Collectibles (metropoliscollectibles.com), an online buyer and seller of vintage comic book collectibles

SportsMemorabilia (sportsmemorabilia.com), a leading provider of sports memorabilia such as baseball, football, basketball, and hockey collectibles

12

COMIC BOOK SALES

If you really love comic books and want to start your own comic book business, why not set up an online business that will not require a major outlay of capital? Starting a business that sells rare comic books over the internet can be inexpensive and very rewarding. You could sell all types of comic books, or focus on Marvel Comics or DC Comics, for example.

For this type of online business venture you can purchase the rare comic books that will be featured and resold on your website from dealers that you meet at trade shows, online, or at comic book stores. You can also offer the opportunity for people to sell their comic books to you via your website. No matter how you go about purchasing them, make sure you have a solid understanding of good-quality rare comic books, so you can sell the best possible merchandise.

If you sell used comic books, you will need an inventory to get started. You will need a copy of a reputable guide that lists the prices of the comics so that you know how much to pay and how much to charge. One thing to remember is if people come to you to sell comics that do have some value, never give them the actual retail value, because this is the way you make your profit. No one will pay more than the price listed in the guides; if you do not leave yourself a margin, you may not make a lot of money.

Place images of each comic book being offered for sale on your website. This will get the attention of a lot of people. Assess each comic's condition, and determine whether your asking price is fair. Also, offer a sampling of the contents of the books you are selling, and as much detailed information that you can provide about each book.

Another approach is to develop the website so that anyone can post a list of comic books for sale, and researchers can come to your site to place an order. All you have to do is process the orders when comic books are sold, and you collect a 10 to 20 percent commission on the selling price of each book. With this approach, you do not necessarily have to have an inventory, because once you receive an order, the books can go directly to the customer from the seller.

Either approach would work well; in fact, there is very little downside to this kind of online business venture. Once established, your business could easily generate full-time income if you do a great deal of promotion, marketing, and advertising in the comic book collectables market.

So what are the best ways to market or promote this kind of site? Develop as many links as possible from websites, directories, and webrings frequented by your target market. Join an online forum to connect with other comic book enthusiasts; just make sure you offer something valuable. You can try launching a strategic display ad campaign on websites frequented by your target market, and also develop a sponsored listings campaign to bid on keyword phrases with the popular search engines.

You also may want to start a weekly or monthly e-letter and send it to your opt-in e-mail list. The e-letter could include news about what is going on in the comic book world, in addition to any new comic books you have in, or a message about an upcoming sale and promotion. You could also launch a blog with similar content.

Finally, collectors enjoying communicating with each other about their comic books; as a result, be sure to set up a message board on your site, where people can communicate about comics and visit your site again and again. Also, try experimenting with social networking tools such as MySpace, Facebook, and YouTube—especially in areas of these sites that discuss comic books.

SKILLS NEEDED

It goes without saying that to be successful in this business, you need to have an in-depth knowledge—actually a love—of comic books. You'll need to know what the latest trends are in the industry, as well how to tell what makes a good rare comic book. Good written communication skills, site design knowledge, good online marketing skills, and great customer service skills are also required.

THINGS TO CONSIDER

If you sell used comic books, make sure to get your hands on a copy of a reputable guide that lists comic book prices so you know how much to pay and how much to charge. One thing you should know is that if people come to you to sell comics that have some value, never pay them the actual retail value, because this is the way you make your profit.

WEB RESOURCES

ComicConnect (comicconnect.com), an online marketplace for comic buyers and sellers

MyComicShop (mycomicshop.com), the world's largest selection of back issue comic books

MidtownComics.com (midtowncomics.com), an online comic book store

Scott's Comics (scottscomics.com), offers more than 100,000 comic books for sale

CONSUMER ELECTRONICS SALES

13

The door is wide open for this type of business, as retail sales for electronic products—including those sold online—continue to soar. Sure, there are plenty of competitors, but if you can find a competitive edge, such as offering a specific type of electronics, you can do a monumental amount of business.

What types of electronics are we talking about? Everything from electronic organizers to large screen plasma televisions is in this category, and they all sell well online. Other gadgets you could sell include video game consoles, personal electronics, and portable media players. As a result of the green movement, there is also a growing interest in buying and selling used or refurbished electronics online.

One reason selling this type of merchandise online is a surefire winner is because people— affluent people in particular—turn to the web to purchase this type of merchandise.

In fact, when it comes to big-ticket items such as plasma televisions and other electronic toys, who actually shops for these items using the web? Answer: The affluent. According to an eMarketer report, households with incomes of more than $100,000 are more inclined to do their research and purchases of electronic goods on the web. The numbers breakdown is clear:

- 93 percent of the affluent research these purchases
- 62 percent used both websites and search engines to conduct this research

- 27.5 percent used e-mail newsletters as part of the research process
- More than half of the affluent buy their computers and peripherals online (59.2 percent for laptops, 61.1 percent for desktops, and 57.2 percent for printers)

What are some techniques to use to be successful in this space? Excellent customer service (online and by phone, if possible), package deals, various perks and amenities, and a wide variety of new and even refurbished products will keep customers and visitors coming back for more.

When selling this type of merchandise, it is a good idea to consider dropshipping, whereby when a customer places an order, it goes directly to the manufacturer or supplier, who in turn ships the product directly to the consumer.

As an online merchant, dropshipping offers a number of advantages. First, and most importantly, you don't have to stock inventory. This means you don't have to rent space to store inventory, you don't have to track inventory, and you don't have to deal with the time and hassle of setting up a shipping department and shipping merchandise to your customers.

Dropshipping also allows you to sell a wide variety of electronics. Because you don't stock merchandise and instead rely upon suppliers and manufacturers to do order fulfillment for you, your online store can carry a wide variety of items. You'll never have to worry about how much of any particular item you need to order, and you'll never have to deal with excess inventory. Reliable dropshippers will fulfill your customers' orders quickly and efficiently, thus enhancing your reputation as an online seller.

Finally, because online merchants who dropship don't have the overhead expenses incurred by merchants that carry inventory, they can pass along the costs savings to their customers. As a result, customers can get terrific bargains, often buying electronics and other items at near-wholesale prices.

What type of marketing would make the most sense here? A subscriber e-mail newsletter perhaps, which offers biweekly or monthly updates of products. Of course, you should also use additional online marketing techniques such as search engine optimization or search engine marketing, as well as other online advertising.

SKILLS NEEDED

You'll need an understanding of the consumer electronics industry, including an in-depth understanding of the products you will be selling, along with an understanding of how the supply chain works. Fulfillment expertise is also important here, as are excellent marketing and customer service skills.

THINGS TO CONSIDER

Either focus on a niche or offer a wide variety of products. If you decide to go the variety route, make sure to keep your prices as low as you possibly can, and, of course, keep focused on great customer service.

WEB RESOURCES

Consumer Electronics Online (consumerelectronicsonline.com), an online seller of audio, video, and home office consumer electronics

Newegg.com (newegg.com), a leading consumer electronics online retailer

onSale (onsale.com), an internet discount retailer of computers, peripherals, software, and consumer electronics to consumers and small businesses; a wholly-owned subsidiary of PC Mall

SonyStyle.com (sonystyle.com), online shopping store for all things Sony

14

COUPON SITE

One area that is growing online today is online couponing; after all, more and more people are trying to find good deals these days, and when you match that concept with the convenience that the internet brings, the result is a win-win for consumers.

In general, a coupon site is a website where consumers can go to view coupons, print them, and then use them in brick-and-mortar stores. These sites can also offer online coupons that give users access to free shipping offers, coupons and discount codes.

For the most part, coupon sites or networks can be targeted at either local or national audiences and can even focus on a specific niche.

How do you make money from this type of online business? Basically, you charge businesses to advertise their coupons on your site. Your job, however, is to promote the site and encourage visitors to use the coupons on your site. In order to get advertisers excited about your site, you have to make sure that a lot of their coupons are actually used. To accomplish this, you will have to test a variety of advertising techniques and see which ones work. When you find the most effective, stick with them and build on your strategy from there.

What kinds of techniques are most likely to produce results? A great place to start is to develop a link strategy by generating links from similar, topic-related, local websites with high traffic, in addition to linking appropriate online directories and as many relevant indices as possible. You also may want to launch a banner advertising campaign on related websites. You can develop a campaign where your banners are the actual coupons from your site. Again, these campaigns need to be highly targeted. You will also want to develop an opt-in e-mail list that enables you to communicate with site visitors, and you should utilize search engine marketing. Try developing a viral marketing strategy where people can send out specific coupons via your site; this will help spread the word as well.

SKILLS NEEDED

Simply put, for this business to be successful, you'll need outstanding online marketing skills. Good written communication skills, site design knowledge and customer service skills are also important. Of course, you must be familiar with coupons, such as which ones are eye-catching and/ or successful and which ones don't usually work.

THINGS TO CONSIDER

Make sure you develop strong relationships with the advertisers on your site and make sure you deliver for them with your marketing expertise, so they will come to rely on you. You may even want to think about implementing a customer relationship management system, although this can be expensive so you might want to wait. It may be a good idea to offer your advertisers guidelines and tips on what makes an effective coupon.

WEB RESOURCES

CoolSavings (coolsavings.com), provider of printable and online coupons

Coupons.com (coupons.com), an online coupon site

FatWallet (fatwallet.com), coupons and cash back offers for merchandise at hundreds of stores

RetailMeNot (retailmenot.com), coupon codes and discounts for 20,000 online stores

15 CRAFT SUPPLY SALES

Many people turn to the internet today to purchase and converse about crafts and crafts projects. It seems as though everybody—from stay-at-home moms to tweens to senior citizens—is getting into the act. What types of crafts are they doing? Everything from carpentry to knitting to pottery, and everything in between. Scrapbooking and card making are very popular right now, in general and online. As a result, a good online business to start is one that sell craft supplies. You could carry craft supplies of every sort, or focus on a niche, such as specialty textiles or pottery.

There are two ways you can sell craft supplies online: the traditional way, where you buy supplies from wholesalers or distributors, gather inventory, and then sell the items on your site. Or you could avoid the costs of maintaining an inventory of craft supplies and instead set up your site so that craft buyers buy from you and the orders are shipped directly from the suppliers. Because there are pros and cons to each method, choose carefully. In the latter case, revenue would be generated by either charging the manufacturers and suppliers of craft supplies a fee for being listed on the site or by retaining a percentage of total sales generated.

There are many opportunities to promote this type of online site. You could promote it by running display advertisements in craft magazines, of which there are many. You could also initiate a direct mail campaign aimed specifically at people in the crafts industry; these names could be gleaned through craft associations, clubs, and even the craft magazines in which you might advertise.

Since crafting is becoming so popular, you also may want to create an online community on your site where people can log on and discuss their current craft projects. This will not only get people to return to your site, but will also offer possible advertising revenue: If you attract visitors to your site, you may have an appealing advertising opportunity for craft supply companies that are looking for a targeted, active, and engaged audience.

You can also offer educational videos or how-to-guides about a certain subject. Knitting websites, for example, work well here, because videos and tutorials really allow viewers to understand the technique. And once they have learned the skill, they will most likely return to your site to buy materials for their new hobby.

SKILLS NEEDED

You'll need an understanding of the crafts industry, including an in-depth understanding of the products you will be selling, along with an understanding of how the supply chain works. Excellent marketing skills and excellent customer service skills are also musts.

THINGS TO CONSIDER

Either focus on a niche or offer a wide variety of products. If you decide to go the variety route, make sure to keep your prices as low as you possibly can, and, of course, focus on great customer service.

WEB RESOURCES

Kaleidoscope Yarns (kyarns.com), a leading online yarn retailer

Craft Supplies Online (craft-supplies-online.com), a discount art supply and craft supply warehouse

The Crafts Fair Online (craftsfaironline.com), a craft supplies portal

ScrapYourTrip.com (scrapyourtrip.com), a leading scrapbooking supply site

16 CUSTOM PRINTED PRODUCT SALES

For schools, churches, sports teams, events, and corporations, custom-printed products are hot. If you want to get in on the highly profitable business of selling custom printing, there are several things you must know, which we will discuss here.

The easiest way to get custom-printed products is to use CafePress.com (cafepress.com), an online marketplace that offers sellers e-commerce services to independently create and sell a wide variety of products; it also offers buyers merchandise in many categories. It has a wide range of possible products such as t-shirts, mouse pads, mugs, tote bags, and key chains. All you have to do is design your pictures or sayings that you want on the items, load them into the site, and start marketing.

Another option is to work with a printer or production business to help you print and fulfill your custom orders.

If you would rather have more control over the entire process, you must purchase special irons, heat presses, or decal material to make different custom printed products. While these machines can be expensive, they will pay for themselves when you begin to sell.

Besides the machines to print the products, you also need transfer paper or decals to use, and the products themselves. Purchasing plain t-shirts, hats, and mouse pads in bulk at wholesale prices is necessary.

There are two methods to building a custom printed product business. The first possibility is to create the custom designs yourself. Many t-shirt sellers do this with cartoon drawings and funny sayings. With this method, you become a product developer and then must find the particular niche or customers to target.

The other method for running a custom printed product business is to print designs that others create. With this model, you will be catering to those who wish to have special t-shirts, hats, or other products for their sports team, school, corporation, or special event. While competition for these may be strong, building a reputation for quality work will increase your opportunities to land new clients.

While many sports teams and schools have a particular mascot and word or words they use on custom-printed products, you can also market your services as a designer. This service can be included in the price or you can market it separately as "design consultation" or something like that.

You also may want to target your printed products toward one particular niche of online customers. You might decide, for example, to specialize in customized items for the workplace that promote a company's URL. Or you might decide to provide unique products for the software industry. Choose a niche that promotes heavily (so it will need your products), has a substantial budget for marketing, and/or participates in trade shows where giveaways are popular.

It is also a good idea to keep yourself up to date on the best deals for the supplies you need and try to arrange for a preferred customer or volume discount with your suppliers.

In some cases, owners of this type of online business do not offer direct sales online; instead, they use their website to promote their products and ask customers and prospects to fill out a form and request a quote.

In other cases, owners have their sites set up to take orders online. Here, they allow customers to upload digital photos, logos, images, text, or anything that they want printed onto merchandise, choose what products or merchandise they would like printed, and then click on a link and order, using PayPal, for example. The custom printed merchandise is sent to the customer when completed. In these cases, some online business owners even offer some already-printed merchandise that people can buy "on impulse."

In terms of marketing this type of online business, develop a link strategy, create great photographs of your products and display them prominently on your website, try e-mail marketing, and make use of search engine marketing and optimization. Create an affiliate marketing program where sites can recommend your service, provide a link to your site, and receive a commission or referral fee every time a customer links through and makes a purchase.

Selling custom printed products can be a lucrative business if you organize and market effectively. Depending on the amount of involvement you want in the process, choose an online fulfillment center or use a local printing company. Otherwise, research printing machines and heat presses and choose the ones that work best for you.

SKILLS NEEDED

Knowledge of the custom-printing industry and an in-depth understanding of graphic design techniques are required. Excellent marketing skills and excellent customer service skills are also essential.

THINGS TO CONSIDER

If you decide to start this type of business, you'll want to either focus on a specific niche or offer a wide variety of products. If you decide to go the variety route, make sure to keep your prices as low as you possibly can, and of course, keep focused on great customer service. Also, make sure to be up to date on the best deals for the products you print on and try to arrange for a preferred customer or volume discount with the printing house you use so you can increase profits. Since customer precuts cannot be returned, make sure to get a deposit with your orders or ask to have them prepaid.

WEB RESOURCES

CafePress (cafepress.com), an online marketplace that offers sellers e-commerce services to independently create and sell a wide variety of products, and offers buyers merchandise across many topics

Collegiate Concepts (imprintitems.com), a provider of promotional products printed with logos that specializes in screen printing, embroidery, and pad printing

Promopeddler.com (promopeddler.com), a leading online provider of custom-printed promotional products

T-Shirt Charity (tshirtcharity.com), a provider of custom printed t-shirts and other products designed for fund raising and brand awareness for non-profit organizations

17 DATING SERVICE

Statistics show that 40 percent of North American marriages end in divorce. While this is a sad commentary on the state of modern-day relationships, it also is an important statistic to keep in mind if you are thinking of starting an online dating service.

While there are many large online dating services on the web today (Match.com and eHarmony.com, as two examples), there is ample opportunity for niche-based dating sites based on interest, gender, graphic location, or even ethnic backgrounds. For example, perhaps you can focus on singles or divorcees in their 50s.

How will you make a profit? By charging a fee for signing up for the service or by offering a free service—but selling advertising space on the site.

While this sounds like a great idea, even if you start a niche service with minimum investment, it is vitally important that you have a business plan and marketing plan in place. After all, many have tried to start this type of business but failed by not seeing the pitfalls along the way. And the number one question you have to answer is "How will I get my members?"

One thing worth knowing is that the bigger online dating sites have a sort of monopoly in the market; thus, they do not always think about things like customer satisfaction, which could be your strong point. They may, for example, continually raise prices; automatically charge your credit card monthly "for your convenience," which makes it harder for you to leave their service; make it difficult for you to contact them; and make it difficult for you to communicate with others by not allowing non-members to respond to paid member inquiries. If you don't do any of these things, your business may have an edge, and you could get some traction via positive word-of-mouth advertising.

Another marketing tactic you could use is public relations: Why not contact your local media and provide them with press releases about your new site and also offer interview opportunities? Go for the local angle when marketing your site. Take out classified ads in your area and when there are enough people signed up there, then think about expanding out. If you cover too large an area too soon, people may not sign up and your member base will take forever to build. By doing local promotions and advertising, however, you strongly build up an area where people can succeed in finding dates, and you can then slowly expand from there.

Another idea to consider is to offer an incentive to sign up. For example, offer an iPod for whoever refers the most new members. Basically, you will want to come up with methods to help people over the hurdle of deciding whether or not to become a member.

Finally, become an expert at the art (or science) of web marketing. To attract members, you need to attract traffic, and one of the best ways to do that is through search engine optimization and interactive marketing.

Also, while privacy issues are always paramount with any online endeavor, they are especially important here. Make sure you plan carefully and use passwords and encryption to protect people's privacy; your success depends upon it.

If you are considering starting your own online dating service business, you need to be careful about screening applications, because countless people lie about themselves online. In addition, since this can be a sensitive subject, you will need to make sure to cover yourself from liability. Create carefully worded contracts that state that you are responsible for linking people through the internet, but once they choose to meet each other in person, you are no longer liable for their actions of activities.

SKILLS NEEDED

An understanding of the online dating industry is a must here, as well as well-developed skills in written communication, interactive marketing, and customer service.

THINGS TO CONSIDER

If you are considering starting your own online dating service business, be careful about screening applications because many people lie about themselves online. In addition, you will need to make sure to cover yourself from liability with carefully worded contracts.

WEB RESOURCES

eHarmony (eharmony.com), a leading online dating website
GreenFriends (greenfriends.com), the world's first, largest and most effective site for singles interested in vegetarianism or environmental protection
Match.com (match.com), a leading dating website
JDate.com (jdate.com), the leading Jewish singles online dating network

DOWNLOADABLE E-BOOK SALES

18

Just as more and more people are going online today—either wired or wirelessly—they are also becoming more and more interested in electronic books, also known as e-books.

Basically, an e-book is an electronic version of a traditional print book that can be read by using a personal computer or by using an e-book reader. (An e-book reader can be a software application for use on a computer or a stand-alone reading device.) The most popular method of buying an e-book is to purchase a downloadable file from a website to be read from a user's computer or reading device. Generally, an e-book can be downloaded in five minutes or less.

Although it is not necessary to use a reader application or device in order to read an e-book (most books can be read as PDF files), they are popular because they have options similar to those of a paper book: Readers can bookmark pages, make notes, highlight passages, and save selected text. In addition to these possibilities, e-book readers also include built-in dictionaries and alterable font sizes and styles.

Typically, an e-book reader (a hand-held device) weighs from about twenty-two ounces to three or four pounds and can store from four thousand to over half a million pages of text and graphics. A popular feature is its backlit screen, which makes reading in the dark possible.

E-books are written on a variety of subjects, from internet marketing to novels. In other words, the subjects are endless. In addition, their prices are comparable to hardcover books.

There are two types of e-books you can sell and market: You can develop your own e-books and allow people to download and purchase them from your site, or you can become a reseller for e-books.

If you are going to resell e-books, you can either become a reseller affiliate for larger sites that already have the books loaded on their server, or you can set up your site so that the books can be downloaded and purchased from your website.

Whichever business model you choose, you probably won't want to start this type of business unless you have an avid interest in reading and the supporting technology needed to distribute e-books.

To market e-books online, it is a good idea to spend time researching where e-book buyers are surfing and then try to become linked on these sites. Of course, you would also want to use search engine optimization and search engine marketing to promote your online business, and you may also want to try setting up a viral marketing campaign where you offer subscribers the chance to "Tell A Friend" about your service via an e-mail message, for example.

You also will want to use targeted online display advertising, develop a mailing list where visitors can opt-in to receive e-mail newsletters (which can also be made available through an RSS feed), get linked from online book directories, or establish links from e-book-related cybermalls and webrings.

But selling e-books is not all. You can gain additional income from selling advertising on your site. In some cases, e-book stores offer their books for free and make money through online advertising. You can also provide an e-book service for authors who want to publish books in an e-book format only. You can market the e-books for them on your site for a low cost to the author. Just think about it: This would give you original content that people would not be able to obtain anywhere else. This is important both from a business perspective and from a search engine optimization marketing perspective.

SKILLS NEEDED

You'll need an understanding of the e-books industry—and of the area of e-books that you are selling. Good written communication skills are must, as well as excellent marketing skills and excellent customer service skills.

THINGS TO CONSIDER

Either focus on a niche or offer a wide variety of products. If you decide to go the variety route, make sure to keep your prices as low as you possibly can, and, of course, keep focused on great customer service.

WEB RESOURCES

Ebook Heaven (ebookheaven.co.uk), a source for science fiction and fantasy ebooks

eBooks (ebooks.com), a leading online source of e-books, with 80,000 popular, and professional and academic e-books from the world's leading publishers

eReader (ereader.com), an electronic book publisher that offers contemporary fiction and non-fiction books, newspapers, and magazines for reading on handheld computers, including the Palm Organizer, Sony Clié, Handspring Visor, and Pocket PC machines, as well as Windows and Macintosh computers

Free-ebooks (free-ebooks.net), a site that lets visitors download unlimited e-books for free

19 EDUCATIONAL PRODUCTS SALES

The sale and promotion of educational products online is a popular and growing business. You can sell anything from books to games to science activities for students. For this type of business, you would target teachers and schools.

Keep in mind, however, that educational products are among the most popular on the internet. But do not let this get you down: as the market expands, quality will most likely decrease. Thus, you can make a real name for yourself by selling only the highest-quality products. Your prices, however, will also have to be very competitive. When setting up this type of online business, the first thing you will want to do is establish a product base and create relationships with suppliers of these products. As for marketing techniques, this type of online business will do well using any search engine optimization/marketing program. Also, you may want to experiment with a comprehensive links strategy, with links being established with affiliated sites and suppliers of educational products. Opt-in e-mail and viral marketing "Tell A Friend" programs would also work well here.

You also may want to get into the social media craze and add real reviews and testimonials from users of the products. Many people today rely on customer opinion instead of traditional marketing materials, especially when researching products as important as educational products. In addition, the potential traffic generated from a product review message board could be spun off into a separate site—or even a special section of your site—where you could sell advertising. You can also expand into another social media technique with this site; for example, you could offer a discussion area for teachers to exchange ideas.

SKILLS NEEDED

It's probably a good idea to have a background in the education market in order to start this type of business. If you don't, it's essential to at least have an in-depth understanding of the education products industry. Good written communication skills are a must, as well as excellent marketing skills and excellent customer service skills.

THINGS TO CONSIDER

In this business, it is imperative that you choose a product base and then clearly define your relationship with suppliers. Also, remember that the content on your site should be geared to the buyers of the products, not necessarily the end user. It is also key that the products you are selling are respected educational tools. Finally, keep your prices as low as you possibly can, and, of course, keep focused on great customer service.

WEB RESOURCES

American Educational Products (amep.com), a leading provider of online educational products

Pearson Education (pearsoned.com), the global leader in integrated education and technology publishing, which offers educational products for children, schools, universities, adults, and corporations

World Book (worldbook.com), the online site for one of the leading educational products in the U.S.

Teacher Created Resources (teachercreated.com), an educational publishing company founded by Mary Dupuy Smith, a classroom teacher

20 FABRIC SALES

Sort of a subset of crafts, many people go online today to look specifically for fabrics. These are used for a variety of things ranging from crafts to clothing to home décor; it is all part of the do-it-yourself generation.

There are several options if you are interested in starting this type of online business. Option one: Develop a portal that brings fabric manufacturers and distributors together with fabric retailers via an online fabric directory website. Worldwide, there are thousands of fabric manufacturers and fabric retailers; as a result, an exciting opportunity exists by bringing these two parties together to buy and sell fabric. In a way it is like a real, online fabric bazaar! In this example, revenues could be earned by charging both fabric manufacturers and retailers a fee for using the directory service.

Option two: Focus on the direct-to-consumer market by creating a website that features a wide variety of fabric for sale. Of course, you could focus on a niche here, such as certain types of fabrics (linen, polyester, rayon, or cotton, for example), or particular categories, such as discount, high-end, apparel, crafting (such as quilting), or home décor fabrics. Potential customers could include hobbiests, fashion designers, interior decorators, and tailors.

The site would be easy to create and should be easy to navigate. It should feature pictures and descriptions of the various fabrics you sell and a price list. Customers can select the fabric they want, add it to their shopping cart, make a payment, and place their order. It is as simple as that.

Promoting the site can be easy: You could initiate a direct mail and/or e-mail campaign aimed at fashion designers, sewing clubs, tailors, interior decorators, or even small, remote communities that do not have a brick-and-mortar fabric shop nearby.

SKILLS NEEDED

You'll need an understanding of the fabric industry—including an in-depth understanding of the products you will be selling and your customer base—along with an understanding of how the supply chain works in the fabric industry. Excellent marketing and customer service skills are also crucial.

THINGS TO CONSIDER

Either focus on a niche or offer a wide variety of products. If you decide to go the variety route, make sure to keep your prices as low as you possibly can, and of course, keep focused on great customer service.

WEB RESOURCES

Fabric.com (fabric.com), a leading online provider of discount designer fabrics

Fabric Depot (fabricdepot.com), the online store for the largest, most complete retail fabric store in the western U.S.

FabricDirect (fabricdirect.com), a seller of finest quality fabrics online at or below wholesale

Reprodepot (reprodepotfabrics.com), which offers a selection of vintage reproduction and retro-themed fabrics, buttons, ribbons, and gifts

21) FANTASY SPORTS SITE

There are millions of fantasy sports enthusiasts on the internet playing for fun and even—in some cases—money. A fantasy sport (also known as rotisserie, roto, or fairy-tale sport, or owner simulation) is a game where fantasy owners build a team that competes against other teams based on the statistics generated by individual players or teams of a professional sport.

Probably the most common variant converts statistical performance into points that are compiled and totaled by the manager that created the fantasy team. These point systems are typically simple enough to be manually calculated by a "league commissioner."

More complex variants use computer modeling of actual games based on statistical input generated by professional sports. In fantasy sports, there is the ability to trade, cut, and sign players, just like a real sports owner.

It is estimated by the Fantasy Sports Trade Association that 19.4 million people age 12 and above in the U.S. and Canada play fantasy sports and 34.5 million people have ever played fantasy sports. In addition, a 2006 study showed 22 percent of U.S. adult males 18 to 49 years old (with internet access) play fantasy sports; fantasy sports is estimated to have a $3 to $4 billion annual economic impact across the sports industry; and fantasy sports are popular worldwide, with leagues for football (known as soccer in the U.S.), cricket, and other non-U.S. based sports.

Fantasy sports sites allow users to create fantasy teams or join them, and often offer news and other information that pertains to the fantasy sport in question. Some sites focus on a variety of fantasy sports, while others focus on just one sport, such as baseball or football, for example.

Setting up a website that handles the statistics of fantasy leagues can be profitable, provided you know all the technical means of gaining the up-to-date statistical information you need. It is time-consuming and not for the faint of heart.

How can you make money from this type of online business? Basically, the leagues pay you a per-team fee to provide the primarily automated statistical service, and you provide the league with pages for each team and central pages for the transactions, league news, and free agents, among others.

As mentioned earlier, there is a steep learning curve for this type of statistical website, but once you establish your site as an excellent service, you can rake in a fortune.

To promote this type of site, make sure you engage in search-engine marketing and optimization and also use e-mail marketing techniques and link building strategies. Of course, if you have a stellar statistical site, your best form of advertising will be word-of-mouth.

SKILLS NEEDED

This business requires an in-depth understanding of a particular sport. Setting up a website that handles the statistics of fantasy leagues can be profitable, provided you are familiar with all the technical means for acquiring up-to-date statistical information. Excellent marketing skills, written communication skills, and customer service skills are also essential.

THINGS TO CONSIDER

This type of site cannot be set up in one day. You'll need a lot of time—not to mention patience—to gather all of the statistical data you'll need. There is a steep learning curve for this type of statistical website.

WEB RESOURCES

Fanball.com (fanball.com), a leading fantasy sports site

Fantasy on Yahoo Sports! (sports.yahoo.com/fantasy) a leading fantasy sports site

Fantasytailate.com (fantasytailgate.com), a fantasy football community with news, cheat sheets, rankings, NFL rumors, mock drafts, and articles

Rotowire.com (rotowire.com), a fantasy sports news site that focuses on MLB, NFL, NBA, NHL, auto racing (mostly NASCAR), golf, college football, college basketball and soccer

FITNESS BOOKS, VIDEOS, AND PROGRAMS 22

The fitness industry generates billions of dollars a year, especially in the area of weight-loss programs.

There are several online approaches you can take in this field. For one, you can start an online business that produces and sells fitness books. You can write the books by compiling information supplied by fitness experts in various fields of expertise. The site can also sell specialty fitness books and videos that you can procure from publishers and book distributors on a wholesale basis. You could focus on fitness in general, or on particular types of fitness, such as yoga or Pilates. You can target it at trainers as opposed to consumers. Or you could focus on fitness for a specific group, such as seniors, skilled athletes, or couch potatoes.

The key is finding materials that are not sold in other retail channels, but this should not be difficult. Fitness is a popular subject, and millions of books on fitness-related topics are sold each year in North America.

Authors, publishers, and video producers could use your site to market their products, which could include everything from books, CDs, and videos to nutritional supplements, exercise accessories, and even online fitness programs that charge a fee for a customized fitness plan tailored to customer needs. In exchange for providing this service, the site could charge these fitness gurus a listing fee to be featured on the site or a percentage of product sales.

How should you market the site? A good idea is to develop a comprehensive link strategy, where you generate as many links as possible from targeted websites and directories. You may also want to participate in newsgroups and opt-in e-mail lists that discuss the fitness industry. Make sure, however, that when you participate in these types of groups, you provide a valuable contribution to the discussion, and make sure to attach your signature with a tagline to all correspondence.

You also may want to publish articles in magazines or e-zines that pertain to this type of business and develop a sponsored listings campaign to bid on appropriate keyword phrases with the leading search engines.

SKILLS NEEDED

You'll need an understanding of both health and fitness issues as well as book, video, and DVD distribution issues. Great online marketing, customer service, and communication skills are also essential.

THINGS TO CONSIDER

The key to this type of online business is to find materials that are not readily available in other retail channels.

WEB RESOURCES

American Council on Exercise (acefitness.org), a fitness industry online resource that also has section on its site that sells fitness books for personal trainers

Centralhome (centralhome.com), a website that sells dance, fitness, exercise and sports videos, DVDs, and books

Collage Video (collagevideo.com), exercise video specialists since 1987

Workout Music Video (workoutmusicvideo.com), an online catalog of exercise videos and music for yoga, Tae Bo, pregnancy, fitness walking, aerobics, and water aerobics

FRESH FLOWER SALES

23

Flowers are a big part of people's lives. They convey a variety of messages perfectly: Get well soon for sick friends and family members, congratulatory messages to a newly promoted colleague, condolences to a grieving family, and love to another person. Every occasion is celebrated with flowers. And online flower shops allow people to send beautiful, fresh flowers easily and quickly—even if they are late to purchase a gift. As a result, selling flowers online can be very lucrative.

There are many types of fresh flowers you can sell online. You can offer a variety of flowers and plants, or focus on a niche, such as "just roses." To be successful in this business, however, you will need to focus on fast and efficient delivery service, and always have an abundant supply of fresh flowers on hand. Because this requirement can be a challenge, you will need to create great relationships with fresh flower wholesalers or a direct grower.

Online florists that offer professionally designed websites that are clean and easy to use will always generate more sales and more traffic than other online florist sites. Since you are selling something that is inherently beautiful, online florist sites should always have an exceptionally good layout and the products and content should be pleasing and inviting.

If you are planning to start your own online florist business, it would be wise to diversify or branch out into other gift areas, such chocolates, balloons, and other novelty items. It is also a good idea to target local corporations, hospitals, and other key potential clients. This will give you an audience that is willing to spend more money then most individual consumers and provide you with repeat business.

What type of marketing should you use? Search engine marketing and search engine optimization are important types of marketing for this type of online business, as are a good linking strategy and a listing on comparison-shopping sites. You also will want to offer an e-mail newsletter to regular customers and be sure to offer specials to these folks, especially around holidays such Mother's Day and Valentine's Day.

SKILLS NEEDED

Of course, you'll need an in-depth understanding of the flower market, including how the supply chain works and what the hottest trends in flowers are. It also would be handy to have an understanding of fulfillment and delivery, since these are key factors in making sure your flowers arrive at their destinations fresh and on time. Excellent marketing, communication, and customer-service skills are all important as well. Also, a great eye for design is important: You need a very attractive website.

THINGS TO CONSIDER

To be successful in this business, you need to focus on fast and efficient delivery service and always have an ongoing supply of fresh flowers on hand. As a result, make sure you create great relationships with fresh flower wholesalers or a direct grower.

WEB RESOURCES

1-800-flowers (1800flowers.com), a leading online flower and gift site
Orchids.com (orchids.com), an site that focuses exclusively on orchids
Proflowers (proflowers.com), a leading online flower site
Wholesale Florist & Florist Supplier Association (wffsa.org), an association of
    wholesale florists and suppliers whose site offers a wholesaler directory

GAMING SITE

Playing games on the internet is no longer a fad; in some cases, it is a way of life. How can you get into the business end of the game? There are two options.

The first is to create the latest and greatest online game and make a fortune selling it. The second is to buy or lease the rights to various online games and offer them on your site. You can make a fortune doing this as well.

Before getting started in this business, it is a good idea to immerse yourself in the gaming world. This will help you determine the game or games that are appropriate for you to sell.

To sell online games, you can offer memberships and downloaded and/or CD versions. You could also offer the games for free on your site and run advertising as a way of generating revenue. If you are selling other people's online games, you can also provide previews, reviews, and trial versions of the games.

You can also run a directory of game sites and charge game developers a fee to list their sites. You could also sell advertising on the site.

SKILLS NEEDED

A love of online games, as well as knowledge of the industry, are necessary. Good online marketing, written communication, and customer service skills are crucial.

THINGS TO CONSIDER

Before getting started in this business, it's a good idea to immerse yourself in the gaming world beforehand. This will help you determine the game or games that are appropriate for you to sell and the audience you need to target.

WEB RESOURCE

Games.com (games.com), a site that offers a variety of free online games

Gameslist (gameslist.com) an online games directory site

Pogo (pogo.com), an online destination with free online games, game downloads, flash games, and multiplayer games

Shockwave (shockwave.com), a site that offers free online games

GIFT BASKET SALES

Online gift baskets? A surefire winner? Believe it or not, yes. Selling gift baskets online is a simple idea for an online business venture that can be very profitable. The best way to make money here is to create a website that features gift baskets for sale aimed primarily at the corporate market.

Keep the site basic by providing perhaps ten or so pre-assembled gift basket options. If you can, try to cover all possible price ranges, such as offering a basic gift basket for $25 and more elaborate or specialized gift baskets increasing in price from there. The increases could be in increments of $10. Prices shown for the gift baskets should be all-inclusive, including delivery and handling charges.

Visitors to the site simply select the gift basket they wish to purchase, enter payment information, and provide the details about who is receiving the basket as a gift. A good way this type of site can be marketed and promoted is by initiating a direct mail and e-mail campaign aimed at corporations, event planners, and real estate agents, since individuals and companies regularly send gift baskets to clients and business associates. The gift baskets can be warehoused in one central location and courier companies can be contracted for delivery purposes.

SKILLS NEEDED

For starters, you'll need an in-depth knowledge of the products you are putting into your gift baskets. Great communication, marketing, and customer service skills are also all crucial.

THINGS TO CONSIDER

If you decide to start this type of business, it's a good idea to keep the site basic by providing a limited amount of pre-assembled gift basket options. If you should also try to cover all price ranges, such as offering a basic gift basket for $25, and more elaborate gift baskets at increases from there.

WEB RESOURCES

Fresh Fruit Baskets (freshfruitbaskets.com), an online store that specializes in orchard fresh fruit baskets

Gift Basket Wholesale Supply (giftbasketwholesalesupply.com), an online directory filled with listings of wholesale gift basket suppliers

Gift Basket Village (giftbasketvillage.com), an online site that offers a wide variety of gift baskets

GiftBaskets (giftbaskets.com), a leading provider of specialty, corporate, or holiday gift baskets

GIFT SHOP

Because of the increasing demands on personal time in today's fast-paced world, more and more people are taking advantage of the numerous opportunities to buy gifts online. Rather than spend precious time traveling to shopping centers and waiting in line, many are choosing the convenience and comfort of shopping for everything from candles to soaps to picture frames from home via the computer. It makes sense; buyers are not limited either by the hours of operation of their local department store or to the items that a particular store chooses to stock.

There are a wide variety of online retailers available via the computer, with many of the most respected names in traditional retailing stepping into the online marketing arena. But your online shop can offer gifts that are original, unique and perfectly suited for the intended recipient, with choices that range from native arts and crafts from indigenous peoples throughout the world to the finest of textiles from the Far East to sleek, modern, high-tech stereo equipment at discount prices. You can offer a wide variety of gifts in many categories or stick with a specific theme, such as gifts for kids, religious events, or socially conscious people.

This type of convenience is especially important around the holidays. Customers appreciate not having to stand in long lines to pay for items or having to carry heavy shopping bags full of gifts through a crowded store. Holidays are also important when it comes to inventory—Mother's Day, Valentine's Day, and Christmas will most likely be your busiest times—so make sure you plan accordingly. By providing a wide range of gift items at reasonable prices, with special discounts, coupons, and perks, your website can be the hit of the holiday. Heavy marketing that features the above-mentioned benefits can pay off, along with good quality products and excellent customer service.

Other marketing techniques to keep in mind include developing a comprehensive link strategy, where you generate as many links as possible from targeted websites and directories. You may also want to participate in newsgroups and opt-in e-mail lists that discuss gifts or include people looking for unique, one-of-a-kind gifts. Make sure, however, that when you participate in these types of groups that you make a valuable contribution to the discussion, and be sure to attach your signature with a tagline to all correspondence.

You also may want to publish articles in magazines or e-zines that pertain to gifts and develop a sponsored listings campaign to bid on appropriate keyword phrases with the leading search engines.

Finally, you would want offer something unique, such as a signature gift box or special gift card from the gifter to the giftee as part of the purchase. With all the online competition out there today, you can never be too unique, customized, or personal.

SKILLS NEEDED

Of course, you'll need an in-depth understanding of the gift market, including how the supply chain works and what the hottest trends in gifts are. Excellent skills in marketing, written communication, and customer service are all important as well. Also, a great eye of design is important—you'll want to have an attractive website that is pleasing to shoppers.

THINGS TO CONSIDER

If you plan to sell a wide variety of gifts on your site, make sure you price them accordingly. If you focus on a niche, pricing isn't as important. Also, be sure to form solid relationships with your gift suppliers—they are your lifeblood.

WEB RESOURCES:

GiftTree (gifttree.com), an online gift shop

MostOriginal (mostoriginal.com), offers unusual gifts, original gifts and unique gift ideas by various artists

Red Envelope (redenvelope.com), a leading online gift shop

Taraluna (taraluna.com), an online site that features fair trade, organic, and green gifts

27) GOURMET FOOD SALES

The Food Network has spawned a generation of foodies who are looking for unique gourmet products. That is why selling gourmet food products online today is a win-win situation.

Maine lobster, French chocolates, and Italian olives are just some of the types of gourmet foods that are sold daily on the internet. Gourmet products are perfect for internet sales because many people around the country do not live near specialty food stores, so they use the internet to find the ingredient or product they are so desperately seeking. In addition, even people who live near gourmet stores often cannot find a particular product they are need and so they turn to the internet. Consumers will pay big bucks for a hard-to-find or unique product—in fact, the more rare or unique the food items are, the higher the profits can be.

What type of gourmet food products should you sell? You could sell a variety of products or focus on one type of product. You could also focus on a specific type of food, such as a particular ethnic food, for example. But when selling this kind of high-end product, do your research and make sure that you are indeed selling high-quality products. People are spending big bucks for these types of gourmet food products so they want to know they are getting the best. And do not lie: If you say you are selling "French chocolates," make sure they are indeed from France; if you miscommunicate on your website, word will travel fast.

One thing to keep in mind: Before choosing a product to sell, make sure you know all about the shipping, handling, and customs rules associated with it. There are often many rules that surround consumable products. In fact, when shipping these types of products to customers overseas, remember that their delivery can be slowed down or stopped completely by customs.

It can also be expensive—or impossible—to work with importers of certain types of gourmet food products, so make sure you have relationships with international suppliers who are willing to export their goods to the U.S. And remember, it can be expensive to ship certain fresh products anywhere; one example is lobster, which you would have to ship overnight to assure that it remained fresh.

One of the best aspects about starting an online business that sells and markets gourmet food is many gourmet food manufacturers and processors will warehouse and drop-ship products directly to your customers. This distribution system is fantastic, as you can save on start-up costs by not having to purchase and warehouse inventory. If you would like more control—or are expanding at a rapid enough pace—you may want to open up a warehouse or distribution center and start shipping and fulfilling products from there.

When you create your website, make sure it has easy navigation, a lot of great product photos, and detailed information about the products, such as their history, or, as we mentioned above, where they hail from. People crave this type of information, in some cases as much as they crave the foods they are buying.

You may also want to think about including recipes on the site, which gives people an opportunity to think about ways they can use the products; it might motivate them to purchase more of the products on your site. It also could be a great way to get repeat visitors, such as by having a "recipe of the week" that appears on the site or possibly gets e-mailed to your opt-in list. Other types of marketing that would work well for this type of online business include interactive marketing techniques such as search engine marketing and search engine optimization, along with display advertising on the right, targeted sites. You may also want to create a paper-based catalog that features many types of gourmet foods and a variety of food producers and manufacturers. Of course, the catalogs should be sent free of charge to potential customers. A catalog, however, can be very expensive to produce. Make sure your site is making a profit before you even think about doing this.

SKILLS NEEDED

Of course, you'll need an in-depth understanding of the gourmet foods market, including how the supply chain works and what the hottest trends in gourmet foods are. It also would be handy to have an understanding of fulfillment and delivery, since these are key factors in making sure your fresh foods arrive at their destinations fresh and on time. Excellent marketing, communication, and customer service skills are all important as well. Also, a great eye for design is important, as you'll want to have a very attractive website that is pleasing and appetizing.

THINGS TO CONSIDER

To be successful in this business, you need to focus on a niche or offer a wide variety of products. Whichever you choose, make sure that you pay attention to quality and only offer the finest products possible. In addition, if you are selling perishable foods, make sure you have a system set up to offer fast, overnight delivery. Also remember that people are not necessarily concerned about price on these types of sites—quality is king.

WEB RESOURCES

ChefShop.com (chefshop.com), an online site that offers a wide variety of products such as fresh produce, chocolates, spices, oils, and more

Earthy Delights (earthy.com), an online site offering wild-harvested and hand-crafted foods, such as wild mushrooms, fine hand-crafted cheese, aged balsamic vinegar, exotic spices, and hard-to-find ingredients from small harvesters and growers

Formaggio Kitchen (formaggiokitchen.com), a site that offers a variety of gourmet products with a focus on artisan cheeses

iGourmet.com (igourmet.com), a leading online seller of fine gourmet foods

28 HEALTH AND BEAUTY AID SALES

Many busy men and women today no longer have time to shop at their local drugstore or chain store for their favorite health and beauty aids. Instead, they turn to their computers and buy these items—everything from perfumes and makeup to vitamins and contact lens solution—online. As a result, with increasing demand for this industry, selling health and beauty aids online offers an excellent online business opportunity.

Since a leading company (drugstore.com) and other well-known general merchandise sites sell most of these items, it is a good idea to focus on a specific type of product, such as perfumes or vitamins, and offer a wide variety of these items. You may want to focus on an even more specific niche, such as "perfumes from France." Another hot area right now—as a result of the aging population—is home health care items. You may also want to focus on selling products not carried by regular vendors, or even products that have been discontinued by manufacturers. You may also think about selling only organic products or target women or men of a specific ethnic group that may have hair or skin needs that differ from the general population.

Before entering this business, it is important to have an extensive knowledge of health and beauty products and of the industry in general. And, for most products, your prices have to be very competitive. An important detail: Do not even think about selling online prescriptions unless you are an online pharmacy approved by the National Association of Boards of Pharmacy.

Marketing techniques that work well for this type of online endeavor include online display advertising on health- and beauty-related websites, in addition to participation in newsgroups and discussion forums in this space. To get people coming back for more, you would want to offer health- and beauty-related articles and tips, in addition to product reviews from customers and manufacturers.

SKILLS NEEDED

An in-depth understanding of the health and beauty market, especially the health and beauty aids that you will be selling, will be necessary. Excellent marketing, communication, and customer service skills are all important as well. Also, a flair for design is important, because you'll need to have a very attractive website.

THINGS TO CONSIDER

To be successful in this business, either offer a specific type of health and beauty product or a wide variety of products. In addition, for most products, make sure to be very competitive in terms of pricing. Do not even think about selling online prescriptions unless you are an online pharmacy approved by the National Association of Boards of Pharmacy.

WEB RESOURCES

Drugstore (drugstore.com), a leading online drugstore and information site for health, beauty, and wellness

Perfume (perfume.com), low-cost designer fragrances, perfumes and colognes

Saffron Rouge (saffronrouge.com), a leading online retailer of organic skincare and aromatherapy products

Vitamin World (vitaminworld.com), a leading online provider of discount vitamins and herbal supplements

29 HOBBY SHOP

While Merriam-Webster defines hobbies as "a pursuit outside one's regular occupation engaged in especially for relaxation," that does not tell the whole story. Hobbies can include everything from collecting to creative and artistic pursuits to sports and even adult education. While engaging in a hobby can lead to acquiring substantial skill, knowledge, and experience, personal fulfillment is the aim.

So what could be more fun than opening an online hobby shop? This truly is a surefire online business idea, because people put a lot of time, money, and effort into their hobbies and spend a lot of time on the internet searching for the products about which they are passionate.

Instead of focusing on hobbies in general, focus on a niche within the hobby sphere. For example, you can focus on stamp collecting, astronomy, or model kits. Revenue for this type of site will come from—you guessed it—sales of hobby products that you purchase from manufacturers, wholesalers, or suppliers. However, you can also make additional revenue through affiliate relationships with manufacturers and distributors of hobby products that pertain to your target market.

Before launching this type of online business, it is important that you fully understand the market you are targeting. This will help you design a website that will insure that visitors return. It also might be a good idea to focus on a hobby that you enjoy, especially since you will be putting a lot of blood, sweat, and tears into making the site work. In addition, you should be an expert on the products you will be selling, since you probably will get inundated with questions once you are up and running.

People love to talk about their hobbies because they are a source of joy. They also like to talk with other people with similar interests. As a result, make sure to have plenty of opportunities on your site for your visitors to communicate with one another. Message boards, chat rooms, and polls are some great ways to do this. You may also want to experiment with advertising or marketing on social networking sites such as MySpace or Facebook, especially in areas of those sites that pertain to your target market.

Other marketing techniques to think about are developing a link strategy, participating in newsgroups and e-mail lists that discuss the type of hobby products you are selling, publishing articles in magazines or e-zines that pertain to your online hobby shop, and developing a sponsored listings campaign where you bid on appropriate keyword phrases with the leading search engines.

SKILLS NEEDED

Of course, an in-depth understanding of the hobby market is key, including how the supply chain works and what the hottest trends in hobbies are. Also, if you are focusing on a specific hobby, make sure you have an in-depth knowledge of that hobby. Passion is also a plus: It would a great idea to start an online business based on your own interest or hobbies. Excellent skills in marketing, written communication, and customer service are all important as well. Also, design skills are important—you'll want to have an attractive website that is pleasing to the eye.

THINGS TO CONSIDER

If you are planning to sell a variety of hobby-related items on your site, make sure you price them accordingly. If you focus on a niche, pricing isn't as important. Also, make sure to form solid relationships with your suppliers—they are your lifeblood.

WEB RESOURCES

eHobbies (ehobbies.com), the leading online hobby shop

Hobbieshobbieshobbies (hobbieshobbieshobbies.com), an online hobby shop that offers radio controlled cars, trucks, boats and planes, as well as trains, models, and collectibles

InternetHobbies (internethobbies.com), an online discount source for thousands of great hobby products from around the world

Old Model Kits (oldmodelkits.com) an online source of rare, out-of-production and hard-to-find kits from the 1930s to the present

HOTEL GUIDE

The travel industry is now one of the biggest industries on the internet. As more and more people travel—and travel frequently—they are looking to the internet to help them plan and book their accommodations. Hotel guides make it much easier for tourists and business travelers alike to do this, so as a result, they are in high demand all over the world.

How does this business work? Like many of the online businesses discussed in this book, you probably will do best by focusing on a specific niche, region, or category of hotels, as opposed to having an all-encompassing directory. For example, you can focus on hotels in New England, bed and breakfasts, or boutique hotels.

Once you've narrowed things down, you will need to build a database of hotels in the area you have chosen. Your site should be set up so hotels can add their listings to your website, and you can build the database from your end. The information about each hotel should include details such as what type of accommodations they have, address, parking, wheelchair access, amenities, number of rooms, nearby restaurants and attractions, and whether they have a pool. You may also provide a form for visitors to send to a specific hotel with specific dates to check for availability. Some hotel guide websites even go a step farther and let visitors book online, either directly from their site or by directing the visitor to the chosen hotel's website.

How will you generate revenue with this type of business? You can charge hotels to be listed on the site, or you can offer the listing for free but charge a fee for a special, highlighted listing. Another tactic is to charge a monthly, biannual, or annual fee for a hypertext link from the database listing to the hotel's website. Finally, you can charge for online display ads on the site.

Travelers love to gather feedback, opinions and information about places to stay from other travelers before making a hotel decision. They also love offering their own opinions. In fact, user-generated content is transforming the internet travel landscape. More and more travelers are saving and sharing travel journals, itineraries, and photos on travel sites— which allows any globe-trotter with an internet connection to become a guidebook publisher.

As a result, if you decide to start this type of business, make sure your site has robust content, such as an area where visitors can rate hotels and leave reviews, as well as a message board that visitors can use to discuss their experiences at hotels mentioned on the site. Articles and reviews about specific hotels you are featuring would also be good. It's important to have great photos and images of the hotels featured on your site; nowadays, people want to know exactly what they are getting before they make a decision about a destination. Another good idea is to feature a new hotel each week and to run contests for free accommodation and the like. All of these things will get people to stay on your site longer— and keep them coming back.

Before launching this type of business, it is important to have a good understanding of the travel industry. Also, remember that this is a very database-driven type of business; you should have great database skills and make sure that your database is updated frequently. Also, make sure to keep in touch with all hotel operators on your site. Contact them regularly to make sure their information is up to date. You can also create a form on your site where hotel operators can update information.

Finally, make sure you have a solid invoicing strategy linked into the database so hotels can pay with a credit card for their hypertext link or enhanced listing.

How should you go about marketing this type of online business? One idea is to develop a comprehensive link strategy where you generate as many links as possible from targeted websites and directories related to your business.

You can also send out an e-mail newsletter weekly that advertises your deals and keeps customers interested in your services. You can even feature a particular hotel each week and charge the hotel for this preferred listing. Or hotels can pay for ads in your e-letter. You may also want to participate in newsgroups and opt-in e-mail lists that discuss travel and online hotels. Make sure, however, that when you participate in these groups, you make a valuable contribution to the discussion, and be sure to attach your signature with a tagline to all correspondence. Publish articles in magazines or e-zines that pertain to your type of business and develop a sponsored listings campaign to bid on appropriate keyword phrases with the leading search engines.

Remember, the hotels that advertise with you rely on you to do a great job of marketing so their sites can be easily found. If you do a good job for them, they will undoubtedly continue to work with you.

SKILLS NEEDED

Before launching this type of business, it is important to have a good understanding of the travel industry. Also, this is a very database-driven type of business; you should have great database skills and make sure that your database is updated frequently. Superb skills in online marketing, written communication, and customer service—for both your visitors and advertisers—are also required. Also, a good graphic design sense is important; you want the pages on your website to pop!

THINGS TO CONSIDER

Make sure to keep in touch with all hotel operators on your site. Contact them regularly to make sure their information is up to date. In addition, make sure your site is interactive and includes an area where visitors can rate hotels and leave reviews, along with a message board that visitors can use to discuss their experience at hotels mentioned on the site, and articles about specific hotels you are featuring.

WEB RESOURCES

Hotels.com (hotels.com), a leading hotel website

Hotel-Guides (hotel-guides.us), an online hotel guide focused on U.S.-based hotels

ILoveInns (iloveinns.com), a bed and breakfast directory site

Si-Mexico (si-mexico.com), an online hotel and resort travel guide for do-it-yourself travel planning anywhere in Mexico

JEWELRY SALES

Because the internet is a great place to reach a worldwide audience of jewelry lovers, it is not surprising that many folks try to sell fine jewelry online.

There is another great reason to sell jewelry online: You can sell high-margin goods that can be stored in small warehouses and shipped more easily than a couch, say, or a cantaloupe.

There are many types of jewelry to sell online. You can sell high-end, expensive jewelry; costume jewelry; secondhand or previously owned jewelry; or handmade jewelry—either created by you or made by other artisans. You can sell all these varieties of jewelry, or you could specialize in certain types, such as diamond rings, watches, or pearl necklaces, for example.

Where to get it? You can get jewelry to sell from a variety of places. If you are selling diamonds on your online retail site, for example, you can work with wholesalers, manufacturers, or importers. If you are selling handcrafted jewelry, you can work directly with artisans, whom you could meet with at trade shows. If you are selling secondhand pieces, you could work with consignment shops or directly with people looking to sell their jewelry. Your site can even offer both services: customers can both sell and buy jewelry from your site.

There are different ways to market certain types of jewelry. Buyers of handcrafted, ethnic jewelry often crave the story behind it: who the artisans are, where they live, and why they became jewelry designers. If your jewelry can be defined as fair trade, which means the artisans are paid what is considered by international standards a fair wage for their work, that information should be included in your marketing materials as it a powerful consumer marketing message these days.

However, there are some generalities when it comes to selling jewelry online. Whether you are selling fine, costume, or secondhand jewelry, the key to making this type of online business work is to have experience in the jewelry business in terms of knowing value, quality, condition, and having overall industry expertise.

You also will need to get exposure. How should you go about doing this? One way is to contact fashion magazines and other publications that your target market reads. Magazines are a good way to market jewelry, because many people make jewelry purchases based on what they see in magazines. You might also consider trying to place your products on cable home-shopping channels, such as QVC or the Home Shopping Network, which are big sellers of jewelry. You should also experiment with traditional interactive techniques such as pay-per-click ads, because search engines are predominantly how people find things for online.

However, jewelry can be a tough sell online, because many shoppers worry about spending too much money on items they can't personally touch and inspect. Therefore, it is important that you have very clear, appealing photographs of your jewelry. This is essential, because people cannot physically pick up the jewelry and the photograph has to tell the story. If you can, find a local photography student that would provide inexpensive images, or, if you can afford it, hire a professional.

In addition, give measurements, or include a commonly recognized household item for scale, so that prospective buyers can judge how big a piece would look on them.

SKILLS NEEDED

Be sure to have an in-depth knowledge of jewelry—including value, quality, condition—and overall industry expertise. Also, understand the best places to procure the jewelry you will be selling, such as wholesalers, manufacturers, artisans, consignment shops, or people looking to sell off their jewelry. Excellent marketing, communication, and customer service skills are essential, and it would help to have some graphic design sense and understand what makes a good photograph and how to make your website appear beautiful and appealing.

THINGS TO CONSIDER

Whatever kind of jewelry you decide to sell, make sure you have high-quality jewelry that is unique, even if it is secondhand. No one wants to be sold junk online!

WEB RESOURCES

American Jewelry Exchange (americanjewelryexchange.com), a site that allows visitors to buy and sell jewelry online

Jewelry.com (jewelry.com), a jewelry comparison shopping site that also offers information about jewelry trends, fashion, and gift ideas

Jewelry Exchange (jewelryexchange.com), one of the nation's leading direct diamond importers and jewelry manufacturers in the U.S.

Zales (zales.com), the website associated with Zales Corp., a leading diamond seller

32 LEFT-HANDED PRODUCTS SALES

Did you know that an estimated 5 percent of the world's population is left-handed, while an estimated 95.5 percent of the world's products have been designed and developed for right-handed people? Smell like an online opportunity to you?

Starting an online business that specializes in selling products specifically for left-handed people is not only a great business venture to set in motion, but also a business venture that makes a lot of sense, given the aforementioned numbers. It also targets a niche, which is very important on the internet today.

Locating left-handed products to sell is not difficult, as there are thousands of manufactures worldwide' that specialize in products specifically for left-handed people.

What are some products that would work in this space? Golf clubs, notebooks, scissors, pencil sharpeners, computer keyboards, pruners, can openers, corkscrews, mugs, and belt buckles, are just some ideas. While there are several online stores and catalogs that already sell many of these products, you can take this idea "up a notch" and sell a particular type of left-handed product—a niche within a niche, if you will. Categories could include sporting goods products for left-handed folks or left-handed products for kids and teens.

In terms of marketing this type of online business, you should use search engine marketing and optimization techniques, in addition to e-mail. You should build a client list and send out e-mails throughout the year offering coupons or sales, and also think about running online advertisements on relevant websites such as those that cater to left-handed people. You also may want to do a direct mail campaign that targets left-handed people.

This type of online site would also do well by experimenting with social media and community marketing. For example, you could start an online forum or community on your site. Here, people can discuss some of the problems they are having in society by being left-handed—it could be one part gripe session, one part dating site, perhaps. In addition, you can include articles written by left-handed people and perhaps list famous left-handed people or create a famous person of the day. You should also think about opportunities for additional revenue here: You could sell advertising on these forums to people interested in targeting this market.

SKILLS NEEDED

Of course, you'll need an in-depth understanding of the left-handed products market. In fact, it may even be helpful to be left-handed yourself (but this is not a requirement). Excellent marketing, communication, and customer service skills are all important as well.

THINGS TO CONSIDER

To be successful in this business, understand that there is a very small universe of people out there that you are targeting, so make sure to spend a lot of time targeting your online business in left-handed newsgroups, for example. You are not looking to reach the masses with this type of business. In addition, while there are several online stores and catalogs that already sell many of these products, you may think about selling a particular type of left-handed product, such as a certain type of sporting goods product for left-handed folks or left-handed products for kids and teens. Also, since there are quite a few left-handed online sites out there, be sure to keep up with your competition, both in terms of setting prices and the merchandise that you offer.

WEB RESOURCE

Anything Left Handed (anythingleft-handed.co.uk), a website for a company that has been a source of left-handed products and information since 1968

Left Handed Golf (lefthandedgolf.co.uk), a site devoted solely to left-handed golf clubs

Lefty's Corner (leftyscorner.com), retail and wholesale left-handed merchandise

The Left Hand (thelefthand.com), an online seller of a wide variety of left-handed products since 1995

MAGAZINE SUBSCRIPTION SERVICE **33**

A great business to start for less than $5,000 involves selling magazine subscriptions online. In fact, this is a good example of an online business that can be started right from your living room.

Currently, there are literally hundreds of magazine and periodical publishers across North America that routinely discount the newsstand price of their publications by as much as 60 percent to enable independent subscription sales consultants (which is what you would be, an online sales consultant) to sell their publications and pocket the difference.

Here is a tip: Practice customer relationship management. Gather information about the people who have bought magazine subscriptions, and build a database of customers that you can target with specific offers about the magazines they are (or they may be) interested in, once you have discovered what their particular interests are.

To make this site work, it is imperative that you offer a large selection of magazines, categorized by demographic audiences (such as boomers and preteen magazines.) If you look for some less popular titles—that is, niche publications—you may even be able to generate a larger audience and more advertisers to the site. You also may want to offer the magazines at lower prices than your competitors. You will make a profit from a percentage of the subscriptions sold. You may also want to try selling advertising on the site.

SKILLS NEEDED

An understanding of the magazine business, including the supply chain, is imperative. Strong online marketing, written communication skills, and customer service skills are also required.

THINGS TO CONSIDER

To make this site work, offer a large selection of magazines, categorized by demographic audiences. Or, if you look for some less popular titles—niche publications—you may be able to generate a larger audience and more advertisers to the site. Keep on top of your competition—and what they are charging. Pricing is very important in this space.

WEB RESOURCES

Carsandmagazines.com (carsandmagazines.com), a website that offers car-oriented magazine subscriptions

Free Construction Magazines (freeconstructionmagazines.com), an online resource that offers free magazines for busy construction professionals

Magazines.com (magazines.com), a leading online discount magazine subscription service

ValueMags.com (valuemags.com), a discounted online magazine subscription service

ORGANIC PRODUCT SALES

Organic products are a major area of growth in our society today. The demand is so high, there is still plenty of room for entrepreneurs to find niches within the wide variety of segments available.

What do we mean by organic products? According to the Organic Trade Association, organic refers to the way agricultural products—food and fiber—are grown and processed. Organic food production is based on a system of farming that maintains and replenishes soil fertility without the use of toxic and persistent pesticides and fertilizers. Organic foods are minimally processed without artificial ingredients, preservatives, or irradiation to maintain the integrity of the food, and agricultural products must meet third-party or state certification requirements to be considered organic.

Organic foods are becoming available in an impressive variety, including pasta, prepared sauces, frozen juices, frozen meals, milk, ice cream and frozen novelties, cereals, meat, poultry, breads, soups, chocolate, cookies, beer, wine, vodka, and more. These foods, in order to be certified organic, have all been grown and processed according to organic standards and must maintain a high level of quality.

Organic fiber products, too, have moved beyond T-shirts and include bed and bath linens, tablecloths, napkins, cosmetic puffs, feminine hygiene products, and men's, women's and children's clothing in a wide variety of styles.

An important part of entering this segment is establishing strong relationships with organic food growers. After forming those connections with suppliers, you will need to create a website that presents organically grown food products, emphasizing their benefits: improved quality and taste while helping to improve the environment (no chemical insecticides, pesticides or other potentially harmful farming practices were used).

Another significant part of this business is online ordering, which provides the delivery convenience that most other retail channels do not offer.

The profit potential in such a business is significant, particularly because organic products can be marked up by 30 to 40 percent. Such a markup still allows a competitive advantage against grocery stores and organic food retailers by 10 percent or more.

Marketing techniques to consider include developing a comprehensive link strategy, participating in newsgroups and e-mail lists that discuss the type of organic products you are selling, publishing articles in magazines or e-zines that pertain to organic items, and developing a sponsored listings campaign to bid on appropriate keyword phrases with the leading search engines.

SKILLS NEEDED

You'll need an in-depth knowledge of all things organic as well as careful buying: you have to have real organic items on your site. Great online marketing, customer service, and communication skills are also integral to your success.

THINGS TO CONSIDER

An important part of entering this segment is establishing strong relationships with organic food growers and suppliers.

WEB RESOURCES

Coco's Shoppe (cocosshoppe.com), an online concept boutique that mingles fashion and beauty care with sustainability and eco-consciousness

Organic Hub (organichub.com), provides links to organic food growers and wholesalers

Organic Kingdom (organickingdom.com), a natural foods online store that carries a large selection of organic products at affordable prices

SkinBotanica (skinbotanica.com), an online store that features a large selection of natural and organic beauty products

35 | PARENTING RESEARCH SITE

Another great online business to start is a parenting research site. What's this? Basically, a parenting research site is an information resource targeted to parents—a group that really craves information.

There are numerous angles you could use to start a parenting site, from talking about vegetarian parenting to launching a site specifically for single moms or gay parents. You can also target a specific geographical area and focus your site on parenting information specific to that area. You should decide whether you are going to target parents of babies, toddlers, preschoolers, children up until the age of nine, tweens, teens, or the whole family. The key is to find a concept and run with it by providing the latest information, stories, and parenting products available.

The site could include articles by experts, chat rooms, discussion boards, forums, and all sorts of content. Keep in mind that this group is exposed to a lot of information, so you need to be clever and build a comprehensive site that reflects the parenting niche market you are trying to reach.

To make money, sell advertising on the site—after all, there are millions of parents out there. If you attract enough visitors, you can make a lot of money through advertising.

As for marketing, a good plan is to develop a comprehensive link strategy, where you generate as many links as possible from targeted websites and directories. You also may want to participate in newsgroups and opt-in e-mail lists that discuss parenting issues. Parents are very active in these types of groups in communities all over the U.S., so this is an especially good technique to use. Make sure that when you participate in these types of groups, you make a valuable contribution to the discussion and attach your signature with a tagline to all correspondence.

You may also want to publish articles in magazines or e-zines that pertain to parenting issues, and develop a sponsored listings campaign to bid on appropriate keyword phrases with the leading search engines.

Finally, you should launch a regular e-newsletter and send it to opt-in subscribers. This group could also receive valuable coupons, sale notices, and free offers from your company and partners.

SKILLS NEEDED

An in-depth-understanding of parenting is an important issue here. It may even help to be a parent yourself, but it is not necessary. Also, excellent online marketing, written communication, and customer service skills are all must haves.

THINGS TO CONSIDER

Before launching this type of online business, make sure you have a target audience and stick with it. New parents have very different needs from parents of teenagers, so make sure you target your content appropriately. This will not only make your readers, but your advertisers, happy. Also, be sure to get as many experts as possible to write for your site; you want to make sure that the information you are offering is correct and from thought-leaders.

WEB RESOURCES

Parentcenter.com (parentcenter.com), a leading online parenting portal that targets parents with kids from the toddler years up to age 9

BabyZone.com (babyzone.com), a leading online parent portal designed to answer baby care and pregnancy questions

CarolinaParent.com (carolinaparent.com), an online resource that focuses on parents in the Research Triangle area of North Carolina (this site is associated with a print magazine)

Robyn's Nest (robynsnest.com), a site devoted to providing parents with the optimal tools to insure the best possible quality of life for their children

PARTY/EVENT PLANNING SERVICE

36

Party planning requires very little start-up money, so it may be the perfect choice for those with no capital. It is also perfect for an online business, because the internet is often the first choice people turn to when looking for a party or events planner.

As an events coordinator or party planner, you will be involved in organizing all aspects of occasions such as anniversary celebrations, family reunions, weddings, retirement parties and baby showers. You could offer both party and events planning services—event coordination usually has more of a corporate focus and involves larger, more complex events than party planning—or choose to do just one. Keep in mind that events may be more lucrative than party planning because of their sheer size. You could specialize in the types of events or parties you plan, such as Sweet 16s, bar/bat mitzvahs, or weddings.

You will be in charge of hiring a caterer, finding the entertainment, creating invitations and party favors, contacting equipment rental companies and choosing the decor. If you specialize in special events such as fundraisers, galas and awards ceremonies, you may also need to handle marketing and accommodations for the visitors.

In most cases, this type of online business is locally based, but if you are asked to plan an event in a location that is farther away, make sure you get reimbursed for the flight and other related expenses.

Decide how you will charge for your services. Most party planners work by the hour or request a flat fee (which can thousands of dollars).

Others charge 5 to 10 percent of the party budget. Your site could also sell party products online.

Before launching this business, consider getting a CSEP (Certified Special Events Professional) certification. It is a great head start if you have no previous experience. In addition, do not start your business by agreeing to plan a large party or event. All the details involved can get overwhelming. If your first or second event is large, consider enlisting the help of a party helper.

In fact, before you even start your business, you may want to team up with an experienced party planner to gain experience and learn the trade before you go off on your own. Alternatively, you can offer your services for free a few times so you can get experience and build a portfolio. Enlist family and friends if you are not confident and then request feedback from them.

You will also need to be familiar with entertainment choices. From karaoke equipment and magicians to disc jockeys and live bands, you should be able to scout out all types of entertainers. Depending on the type of event, you may have to organize tournaments or contests, games and even auctions. Preparing party favors and gift bags may also be part of the job.

When working with clients, it is important to discuss and have a signed contract outlining the services that you will be providing. It is also important that all of your contracts itemize the party supplies, entertainment, food, and drink, among other potential expenses.

Your site should be easy to navigate and full of beautiful photographs. It would be ideal if you could take photographs of the events you coordinate and request testimonials from satisfied clients.

In terms of marketing and promoting your site, make sure to use public relations and word of mouth marketing as much as possible. Send a press release to local newspapers about your online business, for example. Also, create a link strategy where you develop as many links as possible from websites, directories, and webrings frequented by your target market.

You could also try launching a strategic display ad campaign on websites frequented by your target market. These types of sites could include noncompeting party sites, business services sites, and party product directories, to name just a few.

You also will want to develop a sponsored listings campaign to bid on keyword phrases with the popular search engines. You may also want to start a regular e-letter and sent it to your opt-in e-mail list. The e-letter could include seasonal party tips and even a personal journal where you write about some of the recent parties you've planned. You could also launch a blog with similar content.

On a side note, you could start an online directory that includes links to different party suppliers—disk jockeys, caterers, balloon suppliers, audio and video equipment, rental companies and so on—and charge companies for these listings. You can also sell advertising on this site to these types of vendors. You can stick with your local area or offer the service nationwide, where people could type in their zip code and find a variety of choices in their area.

SKILLS NEEDED

If you've hosted a party before—large or small—you'll know that a key skill needed for this type of business is organization. In fact, organizational skills are a requirement. You'll also need great graphic design skills, online marketing skills, written and spoken communication skills, and customer service skills. In many ways, this is the ultimate service business, so be ready to service your customers' needs, no matter what they are.

THINGS TO CONSIDER

Before launching this business, consider getting a CSEP (Certified Special Events Professional) certification. It is a great head start if you have no previous experience. In addition, do not start your business by agreeing to plan a large party or event. All the details involved can get overwhelming. If your first or second event is large, consider enlisting the help of a party helper. Also, when working with clients, make sure to discuss and have a signed contract outlining the services that you are providing, and that the contract itemizes the party supplies, entertainment, food and drink, among other potential expenses.

WEB RESOURCES

Fiesta Gurl (fiestagurl.com), a professional party-planning service in the Chicago area that specializes in children's parties

MyPartyPlanner.com (mypartyplanner.com), a directory of entertainment services online

The Finer Details (thefinerdetails.ca), an online party-planning service in Vancouver, DC

The Party Goddess (thepartygoddess.com), a party-planning service provider in the Los Angeles area

PRESS RELEASE SERVICE

37

Just about everybody likes to see their name, business, or new product or service in lights—or at least on the web. That is why an online press release service can be a very lucrative business opportunity.

Since most people do not have the skills to write quality press releases, there is a need for online press release services that offer, for a fee, writing, editing, consulting, and distribution services for people who would like to get their press releases out to audiences on the web. For example, if you have expertise in the medical or technology fields, it may make sense to focus on writing press releases for those industries.

Some release services offer national online distribution of press releases by partnering with public relations newswires such as PR Newswire. Some offer regional online distribution through major newswires and others use privately collected national sources of distribution. You'll also want to get journalists and other media professionals to join your list so your customers' press releases can be sent to them in an e-mail format as well.

A key issue to think about before launching this type of online business is what type of a distribution agreement do you want to form? If you want to work with major newswires, you'll have to create a great relationship with them, and they can also be expensive. Also, how will you go about gathering the right media professionals to receive your releases? This is also key.

Many services today help their customers make their press release friendly to the search engines by helping them embed hyperlinks and video, and syndicate their customers content with RSS feed and podcasts, among other services.

SKILLS NEEDED

Excellent writing skills, knowledge of press releases and how they work, stellar online marketing skills, and strong customer service skills are all required. It would also be a plus to be web savvy about all the latest-and-greatest web technologies.

THINGS TO CONSIDER

Key issues to think about before launching this type of online business: What type of a distribution agreement do you want to form? And how will you go about gathering the right media professionals to receive your releases?

WEB RESOURCES

24-7PressRelease (24-7pressrelease.com), an online press release distribution service

eReleases.com (ereleases.com), online press release service that offers national distribution

PRWeb (prweb.com), a leading press release service that targets small businesses

Send2Press (send2press.com), an online press release service

PROMOTION COMPANY

38

Another surefire low-cost online business to start is an online promotions company. What is that? Basically, this is a company that puts together promotional campaigns for other businesses. Different types of online promotional techniques include banner advertising, e-mail marketing campaigns, search engine marketing, optimization, and submissions, online contests, online games, live interactive chat sessions, message boards, link strategy promotion, social media marketing, and mobile marketing—just to name a few. While you can focus on a specific region or type of industry to offer your services, the internet allows you to do this type of work for small and large businesses worldwide, so keep your options open.

Before you can even think about starting this kind of company, make sure you have perfected various online marketing techniques so you are truly an expert. You can't just say you are; you have to be able to show it. For example, you should have HTML and graphic design/layout experience, general knowledge of search engines and directories, online marketing and submission experience, and excellent web copywriting skills.

Of course, you can focus on a specific area, such as mobile marketing, or on the whole gamut. You could also think about giving your customers unique offerings, such as geographically targeted or segmented e-mail campaigns. This would not only differentiate you from those offering general e-mail marketing campaigns, it would enhance the professionalism of your online business and position you as a thought-leader or innovator in your field. Just make sure you know what you are doing before you start this up.

Once you have gained exposure, potential clients will visit your site to find out more about your services. You can charge them based on each promotional project you do for their business; just make sure that you study your competitors and offer prices that are competitive.

Always be sure to have a signed contract with your client before you implement any promotional campaign. This will ensure that you receive payment for your efforts. You might also consider a 30 to 50 percent deposit before any campaign is launched. This will provide you with a cushion for your business in case clients default on payments.

Finally, make sure to take the time to plan out all of your campaigns carefully to avoid possible missteps.

What types of marketing programs should you embark on with this type of business? Well, since you are going to be practicing what you are preaching, they better be stellar.

Why not develop a comprehensive link strategy, where you generate as many links as possible from targeted websites and directories? Or you could develop an affiliate marketing program to increase awareness of your business and refer traffic to it. You may also want to participate in newsgroups and opt-in e-mail lists that discuss this industry. Make sure, however, that when you participate in these types of groups, you provide a valuable contribution to the discussion and attach your signature with a tagline to all correspondence. You may also want to publish articles in magazines or e-zines that pertain to this type of business, develop a sponsored listings campaign to bid on appropriate keyword phrases with the leading search engines, launch a strategic online banner campaign, and get listed and linked from internet marketing services directories.

SKILLS NEEDED

Before you can even think about starting this kind of company, make sure you have perfected various online marketing techniques so you are truly an expert. You should have HTML and graphic design/layout experience, general knowledge of search engines and directories, online marketing and submission experience, and excellent web copywriting skills. These skills will are required for marketing your online business as well. In addition, great written and spoken communication skills and great customer service skills are also imperative.

THINGS TO CONSIDER

Always have a signed contract with your client before implementing any promotional campaign. This will ensure that you receive payment for your efforts. Consider a 30 to 50 percent deposit for your service before the campaign is launched. This will provide you with a cushion in case clients default. Make sure that you study your competitors and offer prices that are competitive.

WEB RESOURCES

Grantastic Designs (grantasticdesigns.com), a search engine marketing and design firm

Online-Promotion.net (online-promotion.net), an early pioneer in search engine optimization and online marketing

PureVisibility (purevisibility.com), an online internet marketing company

Search Influence (searchinfluence.com), an economical website promotions firm targeting the small business market

39 REAL ESTATE SITE

With a Google search resulting in 88 million pages for "real estate," it is no wonder that many real estate professionals are building sites. Traditionally, real estate agents would publish their listings in newsletters, home buyer publications, newspapers, direct mail, and on local television. Now they can easily post their listings online to attract a wider audience. Some are posting their listings on online classified sites such as Craig's List and on online newspaper sites, but many real estate agents are setting up their own sites. The area is so hot, in fact, that there are a slew of web design firms that only target real estate agents.

If you are a real estate agent, you could launch a site to target potential clients in a given geographic area. There are even tools designed to make agents' lives easier: HourTown (hourtown.com) is a new online service that allows companies to schedule appointments easily online.

If you are not a real estate agent, another option is to offer real estate agents the opportunity to publish their listings on your site. You can earn a commission from each lead that results in a sale from a referral from your site. You could also work with a web design firm targeting real estate agents; this is a growing area as well.

Before launching this type of business, make sure that all the listings you place on your website are accurate and not misleading. Also, be sure to keep track of your referrals.

Most real estate sites today have gorgeous photography and rich media features that allow people to zoom in and see close ups of homes—or even take a virtual tour of a house. Be sure to incorporate some of these tools into your site. They are relatively inexpensive nowadays.

In terms of marketing, a good idea is to develop a link strategy where you generate as many links as possible from targeted websites and directories. You may also want to participate in newsgroups and opt-in e-mail lists that discuss the real estate industry. When you participate in these types of groups, make a valuable contribution to the discussion, and attach your signature with a tagline to all correspondence.

You may also want to publish articles in magazines or e-zines that pertain cover the real estate industry, and develop a sponsored listings campaign to bid on appropriate keyword phrases with the leading search engines.

You should consider featuring a real estate listing on your site. This will encourage return visits. You can also notify past viewers via e-mail when you update the listing.

SKILLS NEEDED

An understanding of the real estate industry—how it works, major players, etc.—is important, as is great online marketing, communication, and customer service skills. Also, great site design experience is a must: Most real estate sites today have gorgeous photography and rich media features that allow people to zoom in and see close ups of homes they are interested in—or even take virtual tours.

THINGS TO CONSIDER

Before launching this type of business make sure that all the listings you place on your website are accurate and not misleading. Also be sure to keep track of your referrals.

WEB RESOURCES

Agent BizzUp Solutions (agentbizzup.com), a web design firm that targets real estate agents

Homes.com (homes.com), one of the nation's top online web resources for real estate listings

HourTown (hourtown.com), online scheduling software for small business owners

Realtor.com (realtor.com), the world's largest real estate database of homes for sale and the official site of the National Association of Realtors

RECIPE SITE

Just as more and more people are going online today to buy foodstuffs, they are also looking for recipes. As a result, a surefire online business you can start for less than $5,000 is an online recipe site. Cooking recipes, classes, products and ingredients can all be provided and sold via your own recipe website.

There are numerous recipe sites on the web already, so you should specialize by featuring a certain type of cooking, such as organic recipes, vegan recipes, or specific ethnic favorites.

When designing your site, remember that everyone loves to look at gorgeously photographed pictures of food. Spice up your site with food photos and add clever content (such as the origins of the foods) on the site, plus quizzes, contests, and an invitation for people to send in their favorite recipes. You can even build a contest around this by having visitors vote on the best ones.

To get started, first determine the focus and format of the site. There are many choices. The site can provide cooking recipes that can be downloaded for free and supported by selling advertising space and banners. Or you can also make money by selling cookbooks, cookware and related cooking items on the site. A nice touch might be to advertise and promote recipes for a few restaurants, and feature a chef's special recipe.

You can also generate revenue on a recipe website by selling e-books that contain unique recipes, including Amazon affiliate links to your favorite cookbooks along with your own personal reviews of each cookbook, and including affiliate links to online gourmet food stores.

You also may want to participate in newsgroups and opt-in e-mail lists that discuses recipes, cooking, and the food industry. However, when you participate in these types of groups, you make a valuable contribution to the discussion and attach your signature with a tagline to all correspondence.

You also may want to publish articles in magazines or e-zines that pertain to the particular types of recipes and food-related books and equipment you are selling, and develop a sponsored listings campaign to bid on appropriate keyword phrases with the leading search engines.

Finally, it probably would be a good idea to put a message board or chat room on your site so visitors can share recipes and stay on the site longer—which is attractive to advertisers.

SKILLS NEEDED

Of course, a love of recipes is a plus, especially an understanding of the hottest cooking trends. Skills in marketing, written communication, and customer service are all important as well. Also, a flair for design and especially photography is important—you'll want to have a very attractive website that makes the food look mouth-watering.

THINGS TO CONSIDER

To be successful in this business, remember that there are numerous recipe sites on the web already, so you should specialize by featuring a certain type of cooking, such as organic recipes, vegan recipes, or specific ethnic favorites. Also, decide what you would like the format or focus of the site to be. For example, it could provide cooking recipes that can be downloaded for free and supported by selling advertising space and banners, or you could make money by selling cookbooks, cookware and related cooking items on the site.

WEB RESOURCES

All Recipes (allrecipes.com), a complete resource for recipes and cooking tips

Asian Online Recipes (asianonlinerecipes.com), a website that features Asian recipes

Epicurious.com (epicurious.com), a leading online recipe site that features recipes from *Gourmet* and *Bon Appetit* magazines plus web only content and a recipe archive

International Recipes OnLine (internationalrecipes.net), an online exchange group with over 34000 members in 90 countries that offers recipes, a food and wine dictionary, and a bulletin board

41 RECYCLED PRODUCTS

Recycling is not only a good way to cut down on waste and make our environment greener—not to mention reduce our carbon footprint—but it may also be a profitable business.

In fact, there are more and more websites than ever that sell recycled products. Recycled products can include patio furniture, lighting, hammocks, or handbags made from materials such as soda bottles, rubber tires, street signs, copper, recycled paper, and even car seat belts! These types of products are sold by recycled product manufacturers or suppliers.

How can you get into the action? The best way would be to sell a specific type of recycled product, such as recycled bags, recycled apparel, or recycled paper products.

How should you market this business? A good idea is to develop a comprehensive link strategy, where you generate as many links as possible from targeted websites and directories. You may also want to participate in newsgroups and opt-in e-mail lists that discuss this industry. Make sure that when you participate in these types of groups you provide a valuable contribution to the discussion and attach your signature with a tagline to all correspondence.

You may also want to publish articles in magazines or e-zines that pertain to this type of business, and develop a sponsored listings campaign to bid on appropriate keyword phrases with the leading search engines.

SKILLS NEEDED

It goes without saying: Don't even think about starting this business unless you have an in-depth knowledge and understanding of the recycled product industry. Also, for this business, it's important to have good written communication skills, along with excellent online marketing and customer service skills.

THINGS TO CONSIDER

It is important for you to develop good relationships with recycled manufacturers. Also, make sure your products are what they say they are—100 percent recycled—if they are not, and a passionate consumer finds out about it, your business may have to be recycled.

WEB RESOURCES

Abundant Earth (abundantearth.com), a website that offers a rich array of creative and useful products made from recycled materials

Aplasticbag.com (aplasticbag.com), a website that sells non-woven polypropylene bags and totes have the look, quality, strength and feel of cloth

Amazing Recycled Products (amazingrecycledproducts.com), manufacturers and sellers of products made from recycled materials

GreenandMore.com (greenandmore.com), a website that sells a variety of recycled products

42   SCHOLARSHIP DIRECTORY

With the costs of higher education outpacing the rate of inflation, and student loans harder to come by, students are in constant need of sources of academic funds. Every year, thousands of students compete for educational scholarships in North America, and one of the most difficult challenges facing students face is keeping track of the thousands of different scholarships that are awarded each year.

As a result, there is a need for websites that feature information about scholarships and grant awards. These online businesses can help students and their parents learn more about the criteria for receiving such funds. You could focus on all types of scholarships, offer listings of regional scholarships, or list scholarships for specific types of schools, such as technical colleges or graduate schools. Some sites even offer listings of specialty scholarships, such as those for study-abroad programs.

Where would you get this information? In many cases, you will be researching the scholarships yourself. So keep in mind that it can be time-consuming to verify scholarships and other forms of financial aid, as well as refreshing the site regularly so that you have the most up-to-date information possible.

This kind of online business can earn revenue in a few ways, such as charging students and parents a yearly membership fee for access to the site or charging educational facilities and scholarship advisory boards a fee to post their scholarship information on the website. Advertising revenue is another potential source of income as the site grows in popularity and page views.

Market this site in all areas where high school students, parents, and educational institutions can find it. Also, develop a link strategy where you generate as many links as possible from targeted websites and directories.

You may also want to participate in newsgroups and opt-in e-mail lists that discuss scholarships. Make sure that when you participate in these types of groups, you provide a valuable contribution to the discussion, and attach your signature with a tagline to all correspondence.

You may also want to publish articles in magazines or e-zines that pertain to the particular types of scholarships on your site, and develop a sponsored listings campaign to bid on appropriate keyword phrases with the leading search engines.

SKILLS NEEDED

For this business to be successful, it's a good idea to have an in-depth knowledge about all of the different types of college scholarships that are available. It's also important to have excellent written communication skills, along with excellent online marketing and customer service skills.

THINGS TO CONSIDER

Before launching this type of business, consider how you will generate revenue. Should you charge students and parents a yearly membership fee for access to the site? Charge educational facilities and scholarship advisory boards a fee to post their scholarship information on the website? Generate advertising revenue by selling space on your site to companies trying to reach this market? All three? If you decide to choose the latter, consider giving paying customers access to exclusive content.

Also, keep in mind that it can be time-consuming to verify scholarships and other forms of financial aid and you should refresh the site regularly so it contains the most up-to-date information possible.

WEB RESOURCES

FastAid (fastaid.com), the world's largest and oldest guide to private-sector scholarships, graduate scholarships, worldwide scholarships, fellowships, grants; free undergraduate college scholarship database

FastWeb (fastweb.com), a leading online portal that offers financial aid and scholarship information

FindTuition (findtuition.com), a scholarship search service that allows subscribers to search, research, target, and manage scholarship opportunities by specific college, sport, and scholarship type.

StudyAbroad.com (studyabroad.com), a program directory with study abroad information including summer programs and scholarship/financial aid information

SEARCH ENGINE OPTIMIZATION SERVICE

43

As mentioned earlier, search engine optimization is a huge deal. In today's environment, internet sites can only generate traffic if they are heavily promoted and show up prominently on search engines.

While many website operators choose to spend the time doing search engine optimization on their own, many turn to an expert—especially since there are a number of top search engines and each one has a different listing protocol. An SEO expert can help a website appear on the top of the list when users search for a particular term that is relevant to their site.

In short, these businesses help websites enlarge their presence by increasing unique visitor hits, strategically using keywords, and utilizing a variety of other techniques. They then help website operators put these techniques into an overall marketing plan. Some also offer other services, such as search engine marketing and even e-mail marketing.

The best way to promote this type of business? Why, search engine optimization, of course. There are many cyberentrepreneurs who are willing to pay top dollar for such optimization if you are such an expert. But be sure you have the right skills—you really need to be an expert at SEO for this type of business to be successful.

SKILLS NEEDED

It goes without saying that before you even think about launching this type of business, be sure you have excellent search engine optimization skills. And the best way to show these skills off to make sure that your site is at the top of the list when people search for "search engine optimization" in the major search engines. Also, be sure that you have excellent general online marketing skills, as well as communication and customer service skills.

THINGS TO CONSIDER

Before launching this business, make sure to check out the competition. There are many companies out there who now offer SEO services. How will you differentiate yourself? How will you go about pricing your services? These are just some of the things you'll have to think about before setting up this type of business.

WEB RESOURCES

High Rankings (highrankings.com), a leading search engine optimization company

iProspect (iprospect.com), a leading search engine optimization firm

Submit Express (submitexpress.com), offers search engine optimization marketing services and other search marketing services

TopRank (toprankresults.com), a leading search engine optimization and marketing services firm

SOCIAL NETWORKING SITE

44

Just about everybody is visiting social networking websites nowadays. What are they? Basically, a social networking site is an online community of people who share interests and activities or who are interested in exploring the interests and activities of others. The sites also offer a collection of various ways for users to interact, such as chat rooms, e-mail, message boards, blogging, video, and voice chat, among the various communication methods. The main types of social networking services contain directories of some categories (such as former classmates), means to connect with friends (usually with self-description pages), and recommender systems.

Many of the users of communication and content features have come to expect that social networks will include the ability to create personal profiles, share photos and video among online friends, and extend messages or instant messages to other members. On some sites, users can construct public or private discussions around a topic and add tags to their personal journals and photos. If they wish, they can use the network tags to find other members with whom they may share interests or other factors, such as geographic location or having children of the same age.

While there are now many well-known social networking sites such as YouTube (youtube.com) and Facebook (facebook.com), there are still opportunities to start targeted or niche social networking sites/communities.

Before launching this type of business, make sure to find good social networking software that will allow you to set up and manage your online community. The majority of competent social networking scripts are commercial, so you will have to buy them and/or pay an annual subscription fee. At this point you might be thinking "great, where is the problem?" Well, there is no problem; however, since you will have to pay for the software, you had better make a good choice from the beginning.

Most of these products allow you to create your own social community in minutes. You can add a community to an existing website or create stand-alone Web 2.0 site. You can create online networking communities for small groups like school, class, regional groups. It can also be for professional networking or romantic networks. By allowing your users to network with their friends and family, you are allowing viral traffic to your site.

Once your software is installed—which means that basically, your site is up and running—the greatest problem you face will be to actually get people to know the address of your website. It is pretty hard to even get the group of people you are targeting to know about the existence of your website, so this can be a very lengthy and difficult task.

The hardest stage will be the point where the registered people on your website will be you, your good friends, and the good friends of your good friends. Then what? Well, that is pretty much as far as the reaction chain will go, and after that point you will have to do many things to promote your website. Sending a lot of opt-in e-mails will help, as would exchanging links with other websites. Finally, ranking high on search engines would be most helpful, in addition to getting people to spread the word about your website (this last one is a must).

SKILLS NEEDED

Before launching this type of business, make sure you have an in-depth knowledge of social networking. Visit as many social networking sites as you can, and sign up for the ones you find most interesting. Study how they work, what makes them tick, and why people signed up for them.

THINGS TO CONSIDER

Before launching this type of business, make an effort to find the best possible social networking software that you can. This software will allow you to set up and manage your online community, and will form the basis of your business. Most of these products are easy to use; in fact, most of them allow you to create your own social community in minutes. Be sure to make a good choice from the beginning, however, and find software that you are comfortable with, is easy to use, priced right, and scalable. If you have to keep changing your software, it will be headache for you—and your business will suffer for it.

WEB RESOURCES

Facebook (facebook.com), a leading social networking site

Classmates.com (classmates.com), a leading social networking site that allows people to reconnect with former classmates

Grandparents.com (grandparents.com), a leading online community site targeted at grandparents

Naturallycurly.com (naturallycurly.com), a community site targeted at people with curly hair

45 SOFTWARE SALES

Selling software applications offers would-be netpreneurs a very exciting business opportunity. Why? Because worldwide there is a veritable plethora of software designers and manufacturers that produce literally thousands of software applications.

You can sell the same type of software that you'd buy "off the rack" at a computer retail store or allow your customers the ability to download software. You can also try to develop some online software yourself. You can also offer free downloads. With this model, you could sell advertising on your site as a way to increase revenue.

No matter what products you decide to sell, keep in mind that selling software online can be extremely competitive. Consider specializing in one type of software application, such as business-to-business software applications or financial software, for example.

To get started in this type of business, the first step is to secure an agreement with a software developer—or with several developers—to represent and market their products. You can also allow your customers to download the software off your site through agreements with software developers or manufacturers.

In terms of marketing and promoting your business, try using a direct mail or e-mail campaign targeted at the specific group you are trying to reach. You can also register with search engines, link to topic-related sites, use chat rooms, viral marketing techniques, and online advertising programs. Note: This market changes quickly, so make sure you stay on top of the software market to make sure you have the latest products available on your site. As with any online retail business, keep a limited inventory and provide good customer service. In this case, that means you should have a help line available if possible.

SKILLS NEEDED

To be successful in this type of business, it is imperative that you have an in-depth understanding of the online software business, whether you are selling your own software or others. As with most online businesses discussed in this book, it is also important to have excellent written communication, online marketing, and customer service skills.

THINGS TO CONSIDER

This market changes quickly, so it is imperative that you stay on top of the software market and make sure you have the latest products available on your site. As usual, with any online retail business, keep a limited inventory and provide good customer service—which means have a help line available if possible. Also remember that selling software online can be extremely competitive. You should specialize in one type of software application, such as business-to-business software applications or financial software and be sure it is high quality. And, finally, if you are selling software created by software developers or manufacturers, be sure to form good, solid relationships with these parties.

WEB RESOURCES

Download.com (download.com), free-to-try software downloads
Software.com (software.com), consumer software and related information
Softwaresalesonline (softwaresalesonline.com), a provider of current software titles that can be found on retail store shelves
Softwarecasa (softwarecasa.com), a provider of downloadable software

46 SPA DIRECTORY

There are literally thousands of health and beauty spas worldwide that cater to just about any health or treatment need available. As a result, an outstanding opportunity exists to develop an online directory that features world spas.

While a leading online spa site already exists (SpaFinder.com), there are many opportunities to start niche spa sites that focus on specific types of spas, such as medical spas, destination spas, or health spas, for example, or spas in certain geographic locations. If you decide to start this type of online business—niche or not—be sure to index the spas in a variety of ways so people can easily find the listing they want on your site.

How would you make money in this endeavor? Spa operators could pay you a listing fee to receive a headline in the online directory index that is linked to a page that provides more information, such as service provided, location, and contact information. Sales consultants from around the world can be employed by your online business to solicit spa owners to join the directory. The sales consultants could be paid by commission or perhaps with a barter system where they could be provided with free access to a specific spa for a certain number of visits.

How should the site be promoted? Try promoting it via ads in publications or on websites related to health and beauty topics. This is also a great business to promote with public relations. For example, send press releases to editors in the health and beauty industry. You could also use traditional internet marketing and promotional techniques, such as search engine registration and optimization, links, and online ads.

SKILLS NEEDED

An in-depth understanding of the spa business, as well as great online marketing, customer service, and communications skills, are all vital.

THINGS TO CONSIDER

Try starting a niche site focusing on specific types of spas or spas in certain geographic locations. If you decide to start this type of online business, niche or not, be sure to index the spas in a variety of ways so people can easily find the listing they want.

WEB RESOURCES

Destination Spa Vacations (destinationspagroup.com), a site specializing in health spa vacation getaways

Spahub (spahub.com), an online day spa directory

SpaFinder.com (spafinder.com), a leading spa directory site

The Med Spa Directory (themedspadirectory.com), a medical spa directory

47 STOCK PHOTO SERVICE

Stock photos (or stock photography) are professional photographs of common places, landmarks, nature, events or people that are bought and sold on a royalty-free basis and can be used and reused for commercial design purposes.

With stock photography, the photographer (or stock photography distributor) owns the images, and the commercial designer who buys it has some limited usage of the photo. Terms of Service are provided by the company selling the stock photos. Some conditions of use may include that use of the images is licensed, not sold; or in case of a stock photo being used in a magazine, there may be a maximum number of copies of the image allowed to be printed under the agreement. Terms of service policies will differ from one stock photography distributor to another.

In general, stock photography is a cost-effective method for designers to obtain professional photos and images without the costs of hiring a photographer themselves. Stock photos and stock photography refer to the images purchased under this distribution method and may be photos, computer generated graphics, clip art, vectors, and other forms of imagery. Today, stock photos can be purchased through a subscription and downloaded from a stock photography distributor's website or purchased as a CD-ROM collection.

These sites are appealing to beginning photographers, as they provide a great way to get exposure for their work, to improve their skills, and to get to the professional level of selling photographs. These sites typically offer message boards, peer feedback, and charts of which images are selling best. All these sites are free to join and don't charge anything for hosting images. Some of these sites accept and sell only photographs, while others offer vector illustrations and video as well.

Stock photos are used today by newspapers, advertising agencies, marketing companies, publishers, and even individual consumers.

As you can see, an online stock photo service is a great business to start—especially since it can be operated from home on a full- or part-time basis. Another plus: The initial investment is small and the operating overhead is minimal. An online stock photo service allows customers to shop for the photographs they need for a specific project and simply download the files.

It is important to get the word out: You never know when a photograph, even one taken by an amateur photographer, will be perfect for a travel business to use on their website, for example, or a corporation to use in their online annual report. As the owner of the site, you will be responsible for marketing and promoting it and also making sure the photographers are compensated. You will make money by getting a cut of the action for every photo used.

SKILLS NEEDED

In order for this type of business to be successful, it is imperative that you have an in-depth understand of the photography business, along with photography itself. You have to know what makes a good photo, because if the photos you put on your site are low quality, people will notice and not buy. You should check every picture submitted for technical quality as well as artistic and commercial merit. You'll also need good design sense, because you'll want your site to be as pleasing to the eye as possible.

Finally, you'll need excellent written communication, online marketing, and customer service skills.

THINGS TO CONSIDER

If you decide to get into this business, it is imperative that you copyright all of your photographs. Specify the limits to be placed on their use, and make these limits very clear on your site. It's a good idea to build up an inventory of available photos by spreading the word to photographers, both professionals and hobbyists. Online photo stock agencies may sell royalty-free images for as low as $1; the fees on each image are low because the companies sell large volumes of images. The mind set is that quantity will prevail, and the photographers will end up making as much from many small sales as they would from a few large sales through a traditional stock photography business. As a result, if you plan on competing with these agencies, charge a low price, and make sure to get your word out to the masses: both quality and quantity of images will determine how much an artist—and you, if you are selling other photographers' work—will earn.

WEB RESOURCES

Dreamstime (dreamstime.com), a leading stock photo site

Fotosearch (fotosearch.com), a search engine for stock photo images, digital illustrations and artwork, clip art, and stock footage clips

iStockPhoto (istockphoto.com), a leading online stock photo agency

PhotoSpin (photospin.com), an site that offers unlimited high-resolution photo and image downloads for less than a dollar a day

STORE FOR
THE DISABLED

48

With the aging of America, there may be more and more need for online stores that sell products aimed at the disabled or elderly. People with physical disabilities confront challenges in activities of daily living (ADLs), those personal functional activities that are necessary for continued well being, including eating and nutrition, personal hygiene, and mobility. Products in this space assist disabled persons, the elderly, and people with medical conditions and/or injuries.

Products could start with mobility devices such as wheelchairs, scooters, medical braces, and walkers, and can expand to anything that increases independence. For example, some sites sell doorknob turners that enable those with arthritis and similar wrist and hand problems to easily open doors they may have had trouble with before. Others include simple gadgets such as key turners, writing aids, and outdoor tools to make gardening and yard maintenance a breeze.

Such a business can operate well online. After all, many of the people who will be buying these products are homebound and often can't drive or go shopping. You could sell a variety of these products online or focus on a specific niche.

Before launching this type of online business, however, it is important that you understand fully the market you are targeting. This will help you design a website that will entice visitors to return. It's also be a good idea to become an expert in the products you are selling, as you will probably get inundated with questions about the products and their use and effectiveness.

After setting up your site, this business can be capital-intensive, so it is important to develop a well-conceived business plan; however, the profit potential is good, and the business can be personally rewarding.

Marketing techniques to think about when opening this type of online store include developing a comprehensive link strategy, participating in newsgroups and e-mail lists that discuss the type of products you are selling, publishing articles in magazines or e-zines that pertain to the disabled and/or disabled products, and developing a sponsored listings campaign to bid on appropriate keyword phrases with the leading search engines.

SKILLS NEEDED

Before launching this type of online business, it is important that you understand fully the market you are targeting. You should have detailed information about products you are selling and be able to answer questions about their use. As with most online businesses today, excellent marking, communication, and customer service skills are also essential.

THINGS TO CONSIDER

After setting up your site, this business can be capital-intensive, so it is important to develop a well-conceived business plan; however, the profit potential is good, and the business can be personally rewarding.

WEB RESOURCES

1800wheelchair.com (1800wheelchair.com), an online wheelchair store that offers many high-quality discount wheelchairs

Disabled World (disabled-world.com), an international online community for people with disabilities.

Medical Supply 4 U (medicalsupply4u.com), an online shop that carries medical supplies at discount prices

ScooterDirect (scooterdirect.com), senior scooters at discounted prices

TOYS AND GAMES SALES

49

A colorful kid-friendly website is a great—and simple—way for parents and kids to sit down together and create a wish list for Santa Claus, a birthday, or any other special holiday or occasion that merits a gift. While there are many online toy stores out there, you can focus on a specific type of toy, such as dolls, red wagons, or games for "brainiacs." You can also develop your own toys, but that may be something to think about later on.

The best way to market this type of online business is to develop a link strategy, where you generate as many links as possible from targeted websites and directories. You also may want to participate in newsgroups and opt-in e-mail lists that discuss toys, games, and the toy industry. Make sure when you participate in these types of groups, you make a valuable contribution to the discussion and attach your signature with a tagline to all correspondence. You also may want to publish articles in magazines or e-zines that pertain to the particular types of toys and games you are selling and develop a sponsored listings campaign to bid on appropriate keyword phrases with the leading search engines.

SKILLS NEEDED

You'll need an in-depth understanding of the toy business, including how the supply chain works. Great online marketing, communication, online graphic design, and customer service skills are also essentials.

THINGS TO CONSIDER

The toy and game market is not all fun and games. Some people enter this business with the idea that they will be playing with toys all day. While it is more fun than say, selling tires, it is a business, so always keep that in mind.

WEB RESOURCES

eToys.com (etoys.com), an online toy retailer

Fat Brain Toys (fatbraintoys.com), an online retailer and developer of unique specialty toys, games, and gifts

Moolka (moolka.com), an online store that sells imported European toys

Red Wagons (redwagons.com), the leading online seller of Radio Flyer wagons and accessories

TRAVEL AGENCY

50

For next to nothing, you can start a home travel agency in most states. A home-based travel agency is financially and personally rewarding. However, it can be a lot of work. If you can manage time and schedules, starting a home travel agency may be right for you.

Select your target market and decide which travel category will be your specialty. For example, baby boomers tend to travel the most and enjoy taking cruises. Therefore, baby boomers might represent the target market while cruises represent the specialty category.

You can get even more specialized than just cruises, however; think about starting a niche online travel agency, such as one that focuses on adventure travel. Your online agency could offer adventure vacations in hundreds of countries around the world, in addition to being a one-stop resource where customers can research destinations and activities; book tours, airline tickets, rental cars and hotels; and even purchase adventure-related gear, books and merchandise. These sites also contain a strong community element, including trip-by-trip customer reviews and ratings to help others with their trip planning.

Also, think about who you are trying to reach with the adventure destinations you will be featuring: independent travelers or package tourists? Targeting your audience correctly can significantly affect your revenue model.

Before choosing a niche, however, search the web. Select a niche or region and find out what travel websites cover that area. Then think how you can be different from the others and offer a whole different perspective and set of options.

Whichever area you choose, learn as much as you can about your specialty category, but avoid taking expensive courses. Instead, ask suppliers what types of free training they provide.

You will want to set up a website where people can book their own flights, hotels, and cruises directly from providers. Spend time researching the best website hosting deals. Another idea is to visit the QuickBooker website (quickbooker.com), and sign up for an affiliate account. You can set up travel and hotel booking capabilities on your website with their system for free. You will also want to look for other travel and cruise suppliers that offer the same service as QuickBooker.

Design your website to allow customers to book their own flights and to get help directly from suppliers. Provide a customer service number for questions or help with bookings.

Next, you will want to advertise your agency. How should you do this? Hand out fliers and business cards. Submit your website URL to search engines. Buy magnetic signs for your vehicle or place stick-on vinyl letters with your website URL on your rear window. You will also want to use an affiliate marketing program, such as Google AdSense, search engine marketing and optimization, and online display ads.

Also, try partnering with hotels and resorts, and get commissions for any visitors you refer to them. Display a link to their hotel or run a banner ad from them on your site and receive a commission.

Remember, with an online travel agency, content is key. Your site must have gorgeous pictures of the places you will be offering though your agency. Also include great content. Travelers like to know everything they can about a destination before they actually make a reservation.

One way to do this is to create a blog that you can write, and allow visitors to comment on the blog. Be sure to have a message board and chat rooms set up to encourage more dialog. This will surely bring people back to your site.

SKILLS NEEDED

A love of travel is a plus, as is an in-depth knowledge of the travel industry as well as knowledge about the newest trends. A good site design sense is important, as are excellent online marketing, communication, and customer service skills.

THINGS TO CONSIDER

Remember that to start this business, you need to fill out business license applications as required by local, state, and federal agencies.

WEB RESOURCES

Funjet Vacations (funjetvacations.com), a family-owned online travel agency

Just Cruises (justcruises.com), offers knowledgeable cruise agents with a vast knowledge of the cruise industry

The National Association of Commissioned Travel Agents (nacta.com), an association of commissioned travel agents

QuickBooker (quickbooker.com), a service that provides worldwide hotel reservations at all inclusive rates and also offers best hotel deals and hotel search for more than 40,000 hotels

51 WEB DESIGN SERVICE

Just as the online world is growing, so is the need for website designers. After all, their job is to arrange and create the web pages that make up a website. For typical commercial websites, a web designer is responsible for the following:

- **Presentation of the content:** the appearance and information on the site should target the area of the public that the client seeks to attract and be relevant to that audience

- **Usability of the site:** the site should be user-friendly, with simple and reliable interface and navigation

- **Design:** the graphics and text should have an overall professional look and feel that is appealing and consistently flows throughout

- **Visibility:** the site must also be easy to find via most, if not all, major search engines and advertisement media

Web designers are different from web masters in several important ways. The designer should have a creative graphical sense that allows him or her to design a site that is attractive, useful, and representative of a specific product or service. The designer, however, is not usually involved in the marketing aspects of traffic generation on a site—that is usually the job of the webmaster (see page 219).

In order to even start this type of business, you must be comfortable with HTML language and know how to access virtual servers to update clients' websites. You should also be very familiar with graphic design and multimedia programming languages such as Perl and CGI, and database management.

The best way to get the word out about your services is to—of course—create a website that promotes your services. You'll most likely begin your marketing by focusing on your local market, especially as you build your business and try to meet as many people as you can without having to travel. But your business could eventually be nationwide, since most of your services can be done online. You could also target certain businesses, such as law firms, bars, or restaurants, or real estate companies.

You will also want to develop a comprehensive link strategy; that is, get as may links as possible from the appropriate websites, directories, and meta-indexes related to your target market. There are literally thousands of website development-related sites on the internet that would offer a great linking opportunity for your site. It may also be a good idea to develop links from business service sites and directories, which will provide highly targeted traffic to your site.

Another good idea is to participate in newsgroups and discussion forums related to web development and business services. But remember to be careful when using this type of marketing: Only promote your business in the best way possible and only when it is allowed and makes sense. If not, this technique can backfire—and badly—for your business and reputation. Also, when participating in these forums, it is a good idea to use a cleverly designed signature file tagline, as well as a hypertext link that will send readers directly to your site.

You will also want to use search engine marketing, where you can bid on appropriate keyword phrases with the leading search engines. You may also want to engage in search engine optimization and craft your website content so that your site appears on the top of the leading search engine sites when a term related to your business is entered.

Also think about writing interesting articles about web design for e-zines or e-newsletters targeted at potential customers—this will position you as a "thought leader" or authority in your space, which is great from a personal branding perspective.

Along the same lines, think about hosting your own web design advice column for up-and-coming web designers on your site. This would also position you as a thought leader and would be a great way to encourage repeat traffic to your site. What kind of advice should you offer? Anything and everything related to website design, from the best types of software to use for specific web design tasks to specific web design techniques— and everything in between.

SKILLS NEEDED

In order to be successful with this type of business, you must know HTML language and how to access virtual servers to update clients' websites. You should also be expert at graphic design and multimedia programming languages such as Perl, CGI, and database management. Excellent online marketing skills, customer service skills, and communication skills are also key.

THINGS TO CONSIDER

Before launching this type of business, understand that this is very fast-paced. To be successful, you'll have to remain at the cutting edge of all the new technologies that appear, and become expert at them relatively quickly. And keep in mind that the web design industry is fiercely competitive. Make sure you have an excellent portfolio on your site that provides links to the sites you have developed and designed, and include testimonials from clients. This will allow site visitors to assess your work for themselves.

WEB RESOURCES

Falco Design (falcodesign.com), a full service graphic and web design studio

Fry Inc. (frymulti.com), a leading web design consulting firm

Imagn Design (imagndesign.com), a Los Angeles-based web design firm providing website development and design, e-commerce solutions, and custom application development

PaperStreet (paperstreet.com), a web design firm that targets attorneys and law firms

While there are tons of web hosting services online today, there is always room for more, especially since the internet never seems to stop growing.

A web hosting service provides the storage, connectivity, and services necessary to serve files for a website. Web hosts are companies that provide space on a server they own for use by their clients and provide internet connectivity, typically in a data center. Web hosts can also provide data center space and connectivity to the internet, called colocation, for servers they do not own that are located in their data center. Startup web-hosting firms usually sell hosting services from a reseller hosting company to customers at affordable prices.

Before you get started, however, here is a caveat: A web hosting business is not an easy business to run. In addition to extensive computer and technical knowledge, it takes a lot of patience to start and run a successful, solid web hosting business.

First, you will need to choose your reseller hosting provider. This decision could very well be the most important decision you make. Your hosting company will only be as good as the reseller hosting company you choose. This is one of those cases where cheaper is not always better. Make sure your reseller company has live phone support 24/7, rich and robust features, plenty of bandwidth and disk space to start out with and ample room to grow, a good reputation, and years of experience in providing hosting—the longer, the better, in this case.

You will then decide what type of plans you offer. You should offer a range of plans from simple, smaller plans, to medium and high-end plans. However, you should avoid offering too many options. A good number of plans would be three to five initially. Make sure you look at the competition and see what features and prices are being offered. Also, try to find a niche that nobody else is filling in the marketplace.

Next, you need to develop your website. As with most online businesses discussed in this book, good information and an excellent layout are the most important aspects of your site. Make sure your site speaks to your customers' needs. You need to answer one important question that is on your potential customers' minds all the time, "What's in it for me?" You need to spell out for your customers how you are going to solve their hosting needs with affordable, high-quality web hosting and service. In general, use as few words as possible; make sure your main page has at least 500 words but use them carefully. This is important for search engine optimization and marketing.

You also would want to spend time setting up a great support help desk, which is simply a way for your clients to communicate with you about the support they need. Customer service is a key distinguishing factor for web hosting companies: those that provide excellent customer service are successful, ones that do not usually flop. Also, include an FAQ section on your web site or knowledge base to be e-mailed as an auto responder on your support e-mail account. This can help take off the burden of many of these tasks. You might even consider allowing your customers to call you for live phone support.

Finally, you will want to market your site. While time consuming and sometimes costly, effectively marketing your website is an invaluable tool that will keep visitors hitting your site and sales coming in. This is an ongoing effort that takes months and years to perfect. Some directions to consider: current business acquaintances, friends and family, search engine optimization, paid advertising, affiliate programs, and e-newsletters. You also may want to publish articles in magazines or e-zines that pertain to this type of business.

Another good idea is to develop a comprehensive link strategy, where you generate as many links as possible from targeted websites and directories. You also may want to participate in newsgroups and opt-in e-mail lists that discuss this industry. Make sure, however, that when you participate in these types of groups, you provide a valuable contribution to the discussion and attach your signature with a tagline to all correspondence.

SKILLS NEEDED

Do not even think about starting this business unless you have extensive computer and technical knowledge, patience, and excellent online marketing, customer service, and communication skills.

THINGS TO CONSIDER

As was said above, a web hosting business is not an easy business to run. It takes a lot of patience and extensive computer and technical knowledge to start and run a successful and solid web hosting business.

WEB RESOURCES

GoDaddy.com (godaddy.com), a leading web hosting company

HostMonster (hostmonster.com), a leading provider of web hosting solutions

HostNine (hostnine.com), a reseller of web hosting services

StartLogic (startlogic.com), a highly rated web hosting provider

WEBMASTER SERVICE

53

A s the internet grows, so does the need for webmasters. In fact, there is such a need for them, starting up a webmaster business can really be a surefire success.

Basically, a webmaster—also called a web architect, web developer, site author, or website administrator—is the person responsible for designing, developing, marketing, and/or maintaining a website. Webmasters are practitioners of web communication. Typically, they are generalists with HTML expertise who manage all aspects of web operations.

Both large and small companies are looking for webmasters to whom they can outsource. In large companies, there are most likely webmasters on staff, but they often hire contractors on a project basis. Once hired, a webmaster does web design, project management, and updates and maintains a website, or is responsible for specific programs related to the site, such as the affiliate marketing program or the e-mail marketing program. You most likely would be working on a website that you did not build or originate. Webmasters differ from web designers in that they basically run the web operations of a company, versus offering straight design services.

In this type of business, you could have a specific contract to provide services for a set fee, or you may charge by the hour and price your work by the level of difficulty.

In order to be successful—or even start—this type of business, you must know HTML language and how to access virtual servers to update clients' websites. You should also be very familiar with graphic design and multimedia programming languages such as Perl, CGI, and database management. In this type of position, knowledge of internet marketing techniques is a must. You may also be responsible for the passwords for the site, so you would have to be sure to handle this with care, of course.

Before launching this type of business, understand that it is very competitive, especially because entry-level people who will work for very little are calling themselves webmasters. As a result, make sure you accurately define your responsibilities and pricing before launching your business and be ready to explain the value of your services and expertise. Include a portfolio on your site with all of your past projects and include testimonials about your service from your clients.

A good idea is to develop a comprehensive link strategy, where you generate as many links as possible from targeted websites and directories. You may also want to participate in newsgroups and opt-in e-mail lists that discuss this industry. Make sure that when you participate in these types of groups, you make a valuable contribution to the discussion and attach your signature with a tagline to all correspondence.

You also may want to publish articles in magazines or e-zines that pertain to this type of business, and develop a sponsored listings campaign to bid on appropriate keyword phrases with the leading search engines.

SKILLS NEEDED

In order to be successful—and even start—this type of business, you must know HTML language and how to access virtual servers to update clients' websites. You should also be very familiar with graphic design and multimedia programming languages such as Perl, CGI, and database management. In this type of position, knowledge of internet marketing techniques is crucial.

THINGS TO CONSIDER

Remember, in this position, you may also be responsible for the passwords of the site, so you will need to handle this with care.

WEB RESOURCES

The American Association of Webmasters (aawebmasters.com), an association of webmasters

Webmaster Club (webmaster.org), a portal of various websites that provides products and services for webmasters

JX Website Maintenance (jxwebsitemaintenance.com), a provider of premium website maintenance and hosting

One Design Development, (1designdevelopment.com), offers website development, programming, and design

54 WEDDING FAVORS SALES

There are around 2.5 million weddings every year in the United States alone. That is a lot of brides in need of favors and other types of wedding products. In addition, whatever the economic outlook, the wedding industry tends to be secure. As crazy as it sounds, recessions do not adjust people's expectations for their special day. They run up their credit cards and spend their savings on lavish weddings for their children or even for themselves, without ever giving a second thought. Finally, people are usually crunched for time when planning a wedding, so your services can offer them the convenience they're looking for.

These are a variety of reasons why opening an online wedding products business is a surefire winner. Your online business can offer a range of favors such as bubbles, picture frames, and miniature candy containers, just to name a few. You can probably get some good deals from exporters from China; knowing how to speak Chinese is a plus, but not required. You can also specialize in one type of wedding favor, such as engraved items, or focus on unique, elegant gifts. You may also want to expand your business by offering additional related items such as bridal shower favors, bridesmaid gifts, and groomsmen gifts.

You can sell the items online and also offer a value-added service, such as having them gift-wrapped for the purchaser.

Before launching an online wedding favor business, understand that weddings are a seasonal business, so plan accordingly. June is the most popular month for weddings, followed by August and then September.

As a result, you can plan some sort of special promotion to get those July weddings into your business.

Also, the average budget for a wedding is $20,000. That being said, having the ability and the know-how to provide quality favors at a competitive price is going to be very important. So do your homework.

In addition, the average wedding has 175 invited guests, and usually a large percentage of these actually attend. So favor demand should be high for each customer you book. Be prepared to produce not only quality, but quantity.

Eighty percent of weddings are performed in churches or synagogues. Take the time to learn about different faiths and wedding practices so you can customize favors toward your customer's personal views, customs, and beliefs, and you will stand apart from the favor business rat race.

The average couple-to-be spends around $400 on their wedding favors. Multiplied by the 1,772,647 weddings reported in the year 2006, that is $709,058,800 spent annually on favors. So if you can get in on even a fraction of this market, you will have fantastic earning potential.

Keep your site current and your inventory up to date. You will need a clean, easy-to-navigate site with beautiful photographs. You also want to attract as much online traffic to your site as possible. How should you do this? A good idea is to develop a comprehensive link strategy, where you generate as many links as possible from targeted wedding-related websites and directories. You may also want to develop a sponsored listings campaign to bid on appropriate keyword phrases with the leading search engines.

Also, try participating in newsgroups and opt-in e-mail lists that discuss this industry. Make sure that when you participate in these types of groups, you make a valuable contribution to the discussion and attach your signature with a tagline to all correspondence. You also may want to publish articles in wedding magazines.

SKILLS NEEDED

An in-depth understanding of the wedding favor industry, including the supply chain, is key. It is also important to have excellent skills in customer service, online graphic design, online marketing, and communication.

THINGS TO CONSIDER

Before launching an online wedding favors business, understand that weddings are a seasonal business, so plan accordingly. June is the most popular month for weddings, followed by August and then September. Plan some sort of special promotion to get those July weddings into your business.

WEB RESOURCES

Little Things Wedding Favors (littlethingsfavors.com), a site that features unique wedding favors

My Wedding Favors (myweddingfavors.com), a wedding favors site

Wedding Favors Now (weddingfavorsnow.com), a wedding favors site

Wedding Favors Online (weddingfavorsonline.com), a wedding favors site

WEDDING PLANNING DIRECTORY SITE

As we mentioned earlier, there are millions of weddings every year in the United States alone. This, combined with the fact that weddings are recession-proof and that busy brides-to be (and grooms-to-be) regularly use the internet when planning their once-in-a-lifetime event, means there's a great need for web sites solely dedicated to wedding planning resources. The site could be an online directory of sorts, indexed by cites and towns and then broken down into subsections featuring every possible wedding-related product or service including:

- wedding photographers and videographers
- wedding singers, disc jockeys, and musical bands
- wedding planners and caterers
- formal wear and rentals for both men and woman
- limousine services
- makeup artists

Site visitors could simply select the geographic are they are interested in, choose the topic or category of interest, and start to view the information and listings. Anyone getting married would be able to log onto the site and find everything they need to plan the big event.

You could also include categories for specific types of weddings. Here, you could offer a subset of resources specifically aimed at minority weddings or same-sex weddings, just to name a few examples.

Where would you get this information to list? In many cases, you will be finding the information yourself to post. You could find it by searching the internet, through word-of-mouth contacts, or by checking other wedding directories and magazines—both online and offline. Once you get up and running, people may send information to you, so at some point you should include a link on your site that allows this. But when you start out, it will be up to you to get it on your own. Keep in mind that it can be time-consuming to verify the information and refresh it regularly so that you have the most up-to-date information possible. You'll also want to make sure the businesses you are listing are real businesses (and hopefully not fraudulent), so this could take some time.

How would you make money with this type of site? The key way would be through charging for featured listings. These listings could offer clickable links back to the sites of the companies being listed. They also could include a detailed description of the company being listed complete with case studies or a Q and A with the proprietor of it. You could either have the listees write these themselves or you could offer it to them as a value-added service. You might even want to offer the listees the ability to promote videos on your site—and if you have the skills, you could even produce the videos for them as a value-added service. Advertising revenue is another potential source of income, as the site grows in popularity and page views.

Keep in mind, however, that if you can secure even a small percentage of clients out of the thousands of possible listings, you could do very well. The key, of course, is getting the site started, which takes a great deal of research.

Market this site in all areas brides and grooms could find it. That includes running ads in the wedding pages of regional newspapers. Wedding magazines, wedding web sites, and online and offline wedding directories are additional places you could run ads. Develop a link strategy where you generate as many links as possible from targeted websites and directories.

You may want to participate in newsgroups and opt-in e-mail lists that discuss wedding planning. Make sure, however, that when participating in these types of groups that you provide a valuable contribution to the discussion, and attach your signature with a tagline to all correspondence.

You also may want to publish articles in magazines or e-zines that pertain to the wedding planning, and develop a sponsored listings campaign to bid on appropriate keyword phrases with the leading search engines. And, for this type of directory-oriented business, search engine optimization is key.

SKILLS NEEDED

For this business to be successful, it's a good idea to have an in-depth knowledge about wedding planning. Also, it's important to have excellent written communication skills, along with excellent online marketing and customer service skills.

THINGS TO CONSIDER

Before launching this type of business, keep in mind that it can be time-consuming to verify wedding planning information and refresh it regularly. Also, be sure you have a deep understanding of search engine optimization; this will be a key way you will get eyeballs to your site, and the more people that visit, the more advertisers you'll get.

WEB RESOURCES

Best Wedding Sites (bestweddingsites.com), an online wedding resource directory

Wedding Day USA (weddingdayusa.com), an online directory of wedding vendors

Wedding Manor (weddingmanor.com) a site that offers access to wedding professionals

Wedding-Resources.com (wedding-resources.com), an online directory of wedding vendors and services

RESECURCES

Listed below are online resources mentioned in the book. These resources, solutions, and tools will help you as you build your online business.

AFFILIATE MARKETING PROGRAMS
Associate Programs,
  associateprograms.com
Click Booth, clickbooth.com
Commission Junction, cj.com
Commission Soup, commissionsoup.com
LinkShare, linkshare.com

BUSINESS SOFTWARE
Act!, act.com
Microsoft Money, microsoft.com/money
Microsoft Office, office.microsoft.com
Microsoft Outlook, microsoft.com

COMPARISON SHOPPING SITES
AOL Shopping, shopping.aol.com
BizRate, bizrate.com
Google Product Search, google.com/
  products
NexTag, nextag.com
PriceGrabber, pricegrabber.com
Shopping.com, shopping.com
Shopzilla.com, shopzilla.com
Yahoo! Shopping, shopping.yahoo.com

DOMAIN NAME REGISTRARS
Network Solutions Inc.,
  networksolutions.com
GoDaddy Group Inc., godaddy.com
Register.com, register.com

E-COMMERCE RESEARCH
U.S. Census Bureau, census.gov
the e-tailing group, e-tailing.com
Internet Retailer magazine,
  internetretailer.com
J.C. Williams Group, jcwg.com
JupiterResearch, JupiterResearch LLC,
  jupiterresearch.com

E-MAIL SERVICE PROVIDERS/
E-MAIL RESOURCES
Constant Contact, constantcontact.com
Direct Marketing Association, the-dma.org
ExactTarget, exacttarget.com
Federal Trade Commission, ftc.gov
Google Groups, groups.google.com
Topica, topica.com

OFFICE SUPPLY RESOURCES
Nextag.com, nextag.com
Office Depot, officedepot.com
OfficeMax, officemax.com
Staples, staples.com

ONLINE PRESS RELEASE SERVICES
24-7 Press Release, 24-7pressrelease.com
Marketwire, marketwire.com
PRBuzz.com, prbuzz.com
PRWeb, prweb.com

PHOTOGRAPHY/PHOTO EDITING RESOURCES

Adobe, adobe.com
Amvona.com Inc., amvona.com
Apple's iPhoto/Apple's Aperture, apple.com
BigStockPhoto, bigstockphoto.com
Comstock, comstock.com
Canon USA Inc., usa.canon.com/consumer
FotoSearch, fotosearch.com
Getty Images, gettyimages.com
iStockPhoto.com, istockphoto.com
Microsoft, office.microsoft.com/en-us/ clipart/default.aspx
Photography Lighting Company, photography-lighting.com
Shutterstock, Shutterstock.com

PRIVACY SEALS

BBOnLine, bbbonline.com
TRUSTe.org, truste.org

SEARCH ENGINES/ SEARCH ENGINE RESOURCES

Google AdWords, adwords.google.com
Google Inc., google.com
Microsoft adCenter, advertising.msn.com, adcenter.microsoft.com,
Open Directory Project, dmoz.com
Yahoo! Directory, docs.yahoo.com/info/ suggest/submit.html
Yahoo! Search Marketing, searchmarketing.yahoo.com
Yahoo! Inc., yahoo.com

SECURITY SEALS

GeoTrust, geotrust.com
Hacker Safe, hackersafe.com
Thawte, thawte.com
VeriSign, verisign.com

SMALL BUSINESS RESOURCES

Entrepreneur Magazine, entrepreneur.com
Entrepreneur Press, entrepreneurpress.com
FindLaw, findlaw.com
Incorporate.com, Incorporate.com
MyCorporation.com, mycorporation.intuit.com
SCORE, score.org
StartupNation LLC, startupnation.com
U.S. Copyright Office, copyright.gov
U.S. Patent and Trademark Office, uspto.gov
U.S. Small Business Administration, sba.gov

SOCIAL MEDIA TOOLS/SITES

ActiveWorlds, activeworlds.com
Delicious, delicious.com
Digg, digg.com
Facebook, facebook.com
Flickr, flickr.com
Moove, moove.com
MySpace, myspace.com
Reddit, reddit.com
Second Life, secondlife.com
Squidoo, squidoo.com
Stumbleupon, stumbleupon.com
There.com, there.com
Twitter, twitter.com
Yahoo! Search Blog, ysearchblog.com
YouTube, youtube.com

STAT TRACKING SOFTWARE

Alexa, alexa.com
ShinyStat, shinystat.com
StatCounter, statcounter.com

TURNKEY E-COMMERCE SOLUTIONS

1&1 Internet Inc., 1and1.com
eBay Inc., ebay.com
Go Daddy Group Inc., godaddy.com
Google Apps, google.com/apps

Google Checkout, checkout.google.com

Hostway Corp., hostway.com

iPower, ipower.com

Microsoft Office Live,
smallbusiness.officelive.com

Network Solutions, networksolutions.com

PayPal, paypal.com

ProStores Inc., prostores.com

Selling on Amazon, amazonservices.com

Verio Inc., verio.com

Web.com Inc., web.com

Yahoo! Small Business's Yahoo! Merchant
Solutions, smallbusiness.yahoo.com/
ecommerce

WEB RESOURCES

1-800-flowers.com, 1800flowers.com

1800wheelchair.com, 1800wheelchair.com

24-7PressRelease.com, 24-7pressrelease.com

A1 Classic Car Parts Finder,
classiccarpartsfinder.com

AbeBooks.com, abebooks.com

Abundant Earth, Abundantearth.com

Advertising.com, advertising.com

Agent BizzUp Solutions, agentbizzup.com

Alibris, alibris.com

All Recipes, allrecipes.com

Alloy, alloy.com

Amazing Recycled Product,
www.amazingrecycled.com

American Book Company,
americanbookco.com

American Council on Exercise,
acefitness.org

American Educational Products, amep.com

American Jewelry Exchange,
americanjewelryexchange.com

Anything Left Handed,
anythingleft-handed.co.uk.com

Aplasticbag.com, aplasticbag.com

Apparel Showroom, apparelshowroom.com

Art.com, art.com

Artprints.com, artprints.com

Armstrong, armstrong.com

Asian Online Recipes, asianonlinerecipes.com

Auction.com, auction.com

Audiogear.com, audiogear.com

Auto Parts Warehouse,
autopartswarehouse.com

AutopartsGiant.com, autopartsgiant.com

BabyAge.com, babyage.com

BabyBasket.com, babybasket.com

BabyZone.com, babyzone.com

BestBuy Audio, bestbuyaudio.com

BestWeddingSites, bestweddingsites.com

Bluefly, bluefly.com

Buteo Books, buteobooks.com

Burst Media, burstmedia.com

CafePress.com, cafepress.com

Car Finder Service, carfinderservice.com

CarolinaParent.com, carolinaparent.com

Cars.com, cars.com

Carsandmagazines.com,
carsandmagazines.com

Carsdirect.com, carsdirect.com

Centralhome.com, centralhome.com

ChefShop.com, chefshop.com

Cigars International,
cigarsinternational.com

Classmates.com, classmates.com

Coco's Shoppe, cocosshoppe.com

Collage Video, collagevideo.com

Collegiate Concepts, imprintitems.com

ComicConnect, comicconnect.com

Consumer Electronics Online,
consumerelectronicsonline.com

CoolSavings.com, coolsavings.com

Coupons.com, coupons.com

Craft Supplies Online, craft-supplies-online.com

Disabled World, disabled-world.com

Destination Spa Vacations, destinationspagroup.com

Download.com, download.com

Dreamstime, dreamstime.com

Drugstore.com, drugstore.com

Earthy Delights, earthy.com

eBay, ebay.com

eBooks.com, ebooks.com

eBook Heaven, ebookheaven.co.uk

eHarmony, eharmony.com

eHobbies.com, ehobbies.com

eLuxury.com, eluxury.com

Epicurious.com, epicurious.com

eReader.com, ereader.com

eReleases.com, ereleases.com

eToys.com, etoys.com

Etsy, etsy.com

Fabric.com, fabric.com

Fabric Depot, fabricdepot.com

FabricDirect, fabricdirect.com

Falco Design, falcodesign.com

Famous Smoke Shop, famoussmokeshop.com

Fanball.com, fanball.com

Fantasy on Yahoo Sports!, sports.yahoo.com/fantasy

Fantasytailgate.com, fantasytailgate.com

FastAid, fastaid.com

FastWeb, fastweb.com

Fat Brain Toys, fatbraintoys.com

FatWallet.com, fatwallet.com

Fiesta Gurl, fiestagurl.com

FindTuition, findtuition.com

Forcecollectors.com, forcecollectors.com

Free-ebooks.net, free-ebooks.net

Free Construction Magazines, freeconstructionmagazines.com

Formaggio Kitchen, formaggiokitchen.com

Fotosearch, fotosearch.com

Fresh Fruit Baskets, freshfruitbaskets.com

Fry Inc., frymulti.com

Funjet Vacations, funjetvacations.com

Games.com, games.com

Gameslist.com, gameslist.com

Gift Basket Wholesale Supply, giftbasketwholesalesupply.com

Gift Basket Village, giftbasketvillage.com

GiftBaskets.com, giftbaskets.com

GiftTree.com, gifttree.com

Go Daddy, godaddy.com

Grandparents.com, grandparents.com

GreatBaby Products.com, greatbabyproducts.com

GreenandMore.com, greenandmore.com

High Rankings, highrankings.com

Headsets.com, headsets.com

Hobbieshobbieshobbies, hobbieshobbieshobbies.com

HostNine, hostnine.com

Hotel-Guides, hotel-guides.us

HourTown, hourtown.com

HostMonster, hostmonster.com

iGourmet.com, igourmet.com

ILoveInns.com, iloveinns.com

Imagekind, imagekind.com

Imagn Design, imagndesign.com

International Recipes Online, internationalrecipes.net

InternetAutoGuide.com, internetautoguide.com

InternetHobbies, internethobbies.com

iProspect, iprospect.com

iStockPhoto.com, istockphoto.com

JDate.com, jdate.com

JRCigars.com, jrcigars.com

Jewelry.com, jewelry.com

Jewelry Exchange, jewelryexchange.com

Just Cruises, justcruises.com

JX Website Maintenance,
    jxwebsitemaintenance.com

Kaleidoscope Yarns, kyarns.com

Left Handed Golf, lefthandedgolf.co.uk

Lefty's Corner, leftyscorner.com

Lieberman's Gallery, liebermans.net

Little Things Wedding Favors,
    littlethingsfavors.com

Match.com, match.com

Magazines.com, magazines.com

Medical Supply 4 U, medicalsupply4u.com

Metropolis Comics and Collectibles,
    metropoliscomics.com

MidtownComics.com,
    midtowncomics.com

Moolka, moolka.com

MostOriginal.com, mostoriginal.com

MyComicShop, mycomicshop.com

MyPartyPlanner.com, mypartyplanner.com

My Wedding Favors, myweddingfavors.com

National Association of Commissioned
    Travel Agents, nacta.com

Naturallycurly.com, naturallycurly.com

Newegg, newegg.com

Oakwood Worldwide, oakwood.com

Old Model Kits, oldmodelkits.com

Online-Promotion.net, online-promotion.net

onSale, onsale.com

Orchids.com, orchids.com

Organic Hub, www.organichub.com

Organic Kingdom, organickingdom.com

Outside Hub, outsidehub.com

One Design Development,
    1designdevelopment.com

PaperStreet, paperstreet.com

Parentcenter.com, parentcenter.com

Pearson Education, pearsoned.com

Perfume.com, perfume.com

PhotoSpin, photospin.com

PRWeb.com, prweb.com

Pogo.com, pogo.com

Proflowers, proflowers.com

Promopeddler.com, promopeddler.com

Public Surplus, publicsurplus.com

PureVisibility, purevisibility.com

QuickBooker, quickbooker.com

Realtor.com, realtor.com

Red Envelope, redenvelope.com

Red Wagons, redwagons.com

Reprodepot Fabrics, reprodepotfabrics.com

RetailMeNot.com, retailmenot.com

RF Amplifiers, rfamplifiers.com

Rotowire.com, rotowire.com

Saffron Rouge, saffronrouge.com

Search Influence, searchinfluence.com

ScooterDirect, scooterdirect.com

Scott's Comics, scottscomics.com

ScrapYourTrip.com, scrapyourtrip.com

Send2Press.com, send2press.com

Shockwave, shockwave.com

Si-Mexico.com, si-mexico.com

SkinBotanica, skinbotanica.com

Software.com, software.com

Softwarecasa.com, softwarecasa.com

Softwaresalesonline.com,
    softwaresales.com

SonyStyle.com, sonystyle.com

SpaFinder.com, spafinder.com

Spahub, spahub.com

SportsMemorabila.com,
    sportsmemorabilia.com

StartLogic, startlogic.com

StudyAbroad.com, studyabroad.com

Submit Express, submitexpress.com

T-Shirt Charity, tshirtcharity.com

Taraluna, taraluna.com

Teacher Created Resources,
teachercreated.com

The American Association of Webmasters,
aawebmasters.com

The Crafts Fair Online, craftsfaironline.com

The Finer Details, thefinerdetails.ca

The Left Hand, thelefthand.com

The Med Spa Directory,
themedspadirectory.com

The Party Goddess, thepartygoddess.com

Thompson Cigar, thompsoncigar.com

Threadless, threadless.com

TopRank, toprankresults.com

Travel Ad Network, traveladnetwork.com

ValueMags, valuemags.com

Vintage Auto Parts, vapinc.com

Vitamin World, vitaminworld.com

Webmaster Club, webmaster.org

Wedding Day USA, weddingdayusa.com

Wedding Favors Now,
weddingfavorsnow.com

Wedding Favors Online,
weddingfavorsonline.com

Wedding Manor, weddingmanor.com

Wholesale Florist & Florist Supplier
Association, wffsa.org

Workout Music Video,
workoutmusicvideo.com

World Book, worldbook.com

YourBabyStroller.com, yourbabystoller.com

Zales, zales.com

GLOSSARY

Advertising: This is a paid form of communication that allows you to market and promote your products to customers by conveying your exact marketing message. As the advertiser, you have total control over the message, in addition to where and when it appears or is heard. As an online business operator, advertising can be done using many forms of media, including newspapers, magazines, radio, television, billboards and newsletters, and online.

Affiliate Marketing: This type of marketing plan involves getting other online merchants and websites that are not direct competitors, but that appeal to your same target market, to promote your online business by displaying ads or offering links to your site on their site. In exchange, you pay that site either on a per-view or per-click basis, or offer a commission on any sales you generate through a referral.

Blog: A shortened term for a web log, a blog is a website maintained by an individual or company that has regular entries of commentary, descriptions of events, or other content, including graphics or video.

Brick and Mortar Store: Located in the real world (as opposed to cyberspace), a brick and mortar retail store is any traditional retail establishment you'd typically find along Main Street in your neighborhood or within a local shopping center or mall. It can be operated by a local proprietor or be part of a nationwide retail chain.

Business Plan: This is a detailed written document a business operator creates when they are first brainstorming an idea for a new business venture and they are trying to determine whether their idea is feasible. A business plan includes financial projections and forecasts, in addition to a detailed description of the business's goals, strategies, operational procedures, policies and potential.

Cable Broadband Service: A type of broadband internet service with an "always-on" high-speed internet connection. Internet access is delivered through a cable television line that utilizes "shared technology;" that is, all subscribers on the system share a single connection to the internet.

Catalog Page: The part of a website that showcases the specific products being sold. A catalog page can display one or more products at a time and use text, photos, graphics, animation, audio, or other multimedia elements to help sell each product.

Content: The combination of text, graphics, photographs, animations, audio, and other multimedia elements (also called assets) used to populate and create a website.

Conversion Rate: This is the percentage of people who actually make a purchase from your website, compared to the number of people who simply visit the site without making a purchase. As an online business operator, your goal is to create the highest conversion rate possible.

Cost-Per-Click (CPC): How much it ultimately costs for each individual web surfer to click on an online-based ad for a website in order to visit that site. Some online ads are paid for based on the number of people who view them (impressions), while others are paid for based on the number of people who actually click on the ad.

Comparison Shopping Sites: Also known as "shopping bots," these sites are similar to search engines except that instead of finding "information," they are designed to help shoppers find the products or services they are looking for on the internet. Shopping bot sites list specific product information so that shoppers can compare features and prices.

Digital Subscriber Line (DSL): This type of broadband internet service provides "always-on" high speed internet access over a single dedicated telephone line.

Distributor: An authorized representative of a product manufacturer that sells large quantities of a specific product to retailers, who then sell them in much smaller quantities to consumers. As an online business operator, you typically would buy your inventory directly from manufacturers, distributors, importers (if the product is coming from overseas) or wholesalers.

Domain Name Registrar: These are the online-based services, such as GoDaddy.com and NetworkSolutions.com, where someone can register a website domain name.

E-commerce Turnkey Solution: A complete set of website design and management tools that allow anyone to create, publish and manage an e-commerce website for a pre-determined (often recurring) fee. These solutions require absolutely no programming knowledge. A computer with access to the internet is required to use them, because the majority of these tools are online-based.

E-commerce Website: A website designed to sell products online that will ultimately be shipped to the customer once payment is received. Thus, this type of website must quickly and accurately convey details about the product(s) being sold, plus have a shopping cart feature that allows customers (web surfers) to safely and securely place their orders using a major credit card or another online payment method.

E-mail Marketing: This is a type of direct marketing that uses electronic mail as a means of communicating commercial or fundraising messages to an audience. In its broadest sense, every e-mail sent to a potential or current customer could be considered e-mail marketing.

Fulfillment: In the most general sense, fulfillment is the complete process from a point of sale inquiry to delivery of a product to the customer.

Google Checkout: A service of Google, this is a way for e-commerce website operators to quickly and securely accept and process online payments.

Hit: One visitor going to a website or one person viewing a specific web page.

Home Page: This is the main page of any website. It is where a web surfer lands when they enter a website's URL into their browser software.

HyperText Markup Language (HTML): A popular programming language used to create web pages, online documents and websites. HTML defines the structure and layout of a web page and allows for the use of hyperlinks.

Inventory: The amount or quantity of a specific product you have on hand (in your warehouse, for example) to sell to your customers.

Internet Service Provider (ISP): A company or business that provides access to the internet and related services. In the past, most ISPs were run by the phone companies. In addition to internet access, they may provide a combination of services, including domain name registration and hosting.

Logo: A single or multi-colored graphic image that establishes a visual icon to represent a company. A logo can also make use of a specific or custom designed font or typestyle to spell out a company's name.

Mass-Market Retailer: These are large retail superstores that cater to the mass market and carry a wide range of products. Wal-Mart and Target are examples.

Merchant: Someone who sells products or services. In terms of this book, it refers to someone who sells products online using an e-commerce website.

Merchant Account: Offered by a merchant account provider, such as a bank or financial institution, this is what's required for a business operator to be able to accept credit card payments. The merchant will be charged various fees to be able to accept credit cards from their customers.

Meta Tag: This includes specific lines of HTML programming within a website that is used to categorize the site's content appropriately in the various search engines and web directories. In addition to the site's description, title and a list of relevant keywords, incorporated within the HTML programming of the site is a text-based, one-line description of the site (which again utilizes keywords to describe the site's content). A meta tag must be placed within a specific area of the page's overall HTML programming.

Niche Market: This is a narrowly defined group of people that consititute a company's target market. The people in a niche market (or target audience) can be defined by their age, sex, income, occupation, height, weight, religion, geographic area, interests, and/or any number of other criteria.

Payment Gateway: Allows a customer's credit card data to be secure when they are placing orders on an e-commerce website.

PayPal Express Checkout: A service of PayPal, this is a way for e-commerce website operators to quickly and securely accept and process online payments.

Podcast: This is simply a series of audio files that are made available for others to hear. It is called a podcast because it is usually broadcast on a regular basis like a radio show, but listeners have the convenience of listening to the podcast on their computer or MP3 player, such as an iPod. Another feature of a podcast is that its availability is often announced via RSS feed. [See RSS Feed]

Product: The specific items an online business operator will be selling.

Public Relations: A marketing strategy used to obtain free editorial coverage in the media in the form of product reviews, interviews, and/or product mentions in news stories, for example.

Retail Price: This is the price that a merchant (retailer or online business operator) sets on a specific product.

Really Simple Syndication (RSS) feed: A web feed that automatically delivers updated digital content to subscribers; examples are blog entries, news headlines, or podcasts.

Search Engine: A comprehensive and ever-growing listing or directory of websites and their content.

Search Engine Marketing (also referred to as **keyword advertising**): A form of internet marketing that seeks to promote websites by increasing their visibility in search engine result pages. It involves paid, keyword (text-based) advertising that uses Yahoo Search

Engine Marketing, Google AdWords, and/or Microsoft AdCenter. This helps to drive very targeted traffic to a site easily and inexpensively. These short, text-only ads are keyword-based and appear when a potential customer enters a specific search phrase into a search engine, for example.

Search Engine Optimization (SEO): is the process of improving the volume and quality of traffic to a web site from search engines via "natural" ("organic" or "algorithmic") search results. This involves getting your site listed with the major search engines, like Yahoo! and Google, and then working to constantly maintain and improve your ranking and positioning with each search engine, so that your site is easy to find and receives top placement.

Secure Sockets Layer (SSL) Encryption: The technology used to allow safe and secure online credit card transactions (payments) through the internet. Proper encryption helps to prevent hackers from obtaining customers' credit card data and personal information, which could then be used to commit fraud or other crimes. SSL is used for transmitting data securely over the web.

Shopping Cart: The module of an e-commerce website that serves as an interactive order form. It allows customers to input their order, shipping details and credit card/payment information in a secure manner, and then place their order electronically through a website.

Social Media Marketing: A type of internet marketing that seeks to achieve branding and marketing communication goals through participation in social media networks. The central theme of these sites is user-generated content with the social aspects of allowing users to set up communities, invite friends, and share common interests.

Target Audience: This is the core group of people a business's products will most appeal to and who will comprise a product's core customer base.

Traffic: Refers to the number of web surfers who visit site on an hourly, daily, weekly, monthly or annual basis. A visitor is someone who surfs over to a website to explore. The goal of an online merchant is to transform web surfers into paying customers who ultimately place orders for products electronically when visiting a site.

URL (Uniform Resource Locators): A website address. A typical URL has three main components. The first part, the Protocol Identifier, typically begins with "http://". The second part of a URL, the resource name, specifies the IP address or domain name where the resource is located. The third part of a URL is its extension, which typically ".com", although a variety of other extensions are available, such as .edu, .org, .net., .gov, .info, .TV, .biz, .name and .us.

Virtual Worlds: These are computer-based simulated environments intended for their users to inhabit and interact via avatars (their virtual representations of themselves). Many marketers use these worlds to promote products and services.

Web Browser: The software used by web surfers to surf the web. Internet Explorer, Safari, and Firefox are examples of popular web browsers. When creating an online-based business, it is essential that the website be compatible with all of the popular browsers.

Web Page: A text document that usually includes formatting and links to other pages. This special formatting is called tags, which are part of HTML and are used to link one page, section or image to another.

Website Template: Offered by e-commerce turnkey solutions, these are standard web page or overall web site designs that were created by professional designers, artists, and/or programmers and can be fully customized to create a unique website.

Wholesale Price: The discounted price a merchant pays to purchase products in quantity from a wholesaler or distributor. Once products are acquired for resale, the merchant then marks up the price and they are sold to customers at a retail price. Part of the profit is calculated based on the difference between the wholesale price of a product and the price at which it it sold. All of the other business operating expenses, however, must also be taken into account when calculating profits.

Widgets: Also called gadgets, widgets are like mini television screens that contain information such as a brand, logo, or any interesting information that pertains to a brand that can be posted on a website, blog, or desktop. Visitors to a website with a widget on it will see it, download it, and post it on their own blogs or other sites.

Wiki: A wiki is a collection of web pages designed to enable anyone who accesses it to contribute or modify content, using a simplified mark-up language. Wikis are often used to create collaborative websites and to power community websites.

INDEX